CINCINNATI Christmas

CINCINNATI
Christmas

HISTORY · TRADITION · FOOD

Jinny Powers Berten

ORANGE *frazer* PRESS
Wilmington, Ohio

ISBN 978-1933197-869

Copyright©2011 Jinny Powers Berten

Additional copies of *Cincinnati Christmas: History, Tradition, Food* may be ordered directly from:

Orange Frazer Press   Fountain Square Publishing
P.O. Box 214   or   fspcincinnati@aol.com
Wilmington, OH 45177   bertenjs@msn.com
800.852.9332   513-961-6762
www.orangefrazer.com
www.orangefrazercustombooks.com

Book and cover design: Chad DeBoard, Orange Frazer Press

The font used in this book was inspired by the handwriting of Nicholas Longworth (1783-1863) from a letter he wrote in Cincinnati, dated January 3, 1816.

Library of Congress Control Number: 2011933092

Printed in China

Dedication

To all the people in the Cincinnati area who work on their Christmas holiday so that the rest of us are free to celebrate with our families in peace and security. They are truly the Christmas spirits.

To Kent,
Merry Christmas!
Jimmy Berten
2011

Table of Contents

Acknowledgements

So many people helped create this book. They gave direction, information, criticism, humor and encouragement.

This book would not have happened without the encouragement and enthusiasm of photographer Robert Flischel. His ability to catch the light and the moment brings the spirit of his "lovable old river town" at Christmas to life and delivers the joy of the season. Thank you and thank you again. And thank you also to his assistant, Mara Mulvihill, who patiently took many messages and answered questions.

Many thanks to all the librarians at the Cincinnati Historical Society Library who patiently helped the search, especially Anne Shepherd and Barbara Dawson. Thanks also to Christine Engels and Linda Baily who gave guidance. Thank you to Stephen Headley at the Cincinnati Public Library and all the folks in the library's Cincinnati Room. Jonathan Nolting at the Cincinnati Art Museum was a great help in providing pictures of the Cincinnati treasures at the museum, and Amy Dehan found just the right items. Ed Rider and Diane Brown at Procter & Gamble graciously opened the archives and permitted us to take pictures. Julie Cornwall at Scripps helped with permissions.

Thanks also to Dr. Jim Hanson at the Museum of Fur, Sarah Siegrist at the Behringer-Crawford Museum, Kathleen Romero at the James A. Ramage Civil War Museum and Mack McCormick at the University Press of Kentucky.

Dotty Weil led me to her brother's "Christmas on the River" which is just what I was looking for.

Books don't become books without editors and readers to polish and polish the many words that land in the manuscript. Sandy Cohan, Anne Montague and Peggy Bertelsman did just that with patience and humor. They deserve thanks, Christmas thanks. Words don't land in my manuscripts without the help of a talented typist whose fingers can fly. Pam Kozma's fingers fly and I am so grateful that they do.

A special thanks to Robert Wimberg for reading the manuscript to confirm the accuracy of the history.

Jody Biedenharn, Phil Nuxhall, James Brock and Rob Barber helped in special ways.

So many people helped with pictures: Pita Niehaus from Graeter's, Nancy Hundrup from Servatii's, Maureen Arat at the BonBonerie, Stacey Recht and Peter Mueller at the Cincinnati Ballet.

Melissa Mileto at Take the Cake, Christy Samad at 3CDC, Emily Johnson at Downtown Cincinnati, Marcia Blust from the Cincinnati Boys Choir, Emma Caro at Playhouse in the Park, Jill Cahill at St. Ursula Academy, Conkie Greiwe at Summit Country Day School, Laureen Hess at the May Festival, Tom Wolfe and Chris Hamerick at Duke Energy, Amy Lorenson and Bob Beiring for The Boar's Head Festival, Andrea Schepmann and Gary Kessler at the Krohn, Adrienne Sedgwick at the Cincinnati Museum Center, Kelly Riccetti for her great pictures of the crib in Eden Park, Riley Humler and Randy Sandler.

The creative, kind, patient and capable folks at Orange Frazer Press are the best. Sarah Hawley, Janice Ellis, Chad DeBoard, Marcy Hawley, and John Baskin took me by the hand and made a book. Thank you so very much.

And thanks to our daughter, Kate, whose patience and clear instructions led me through the maze of computer questions.

Much support and understanding came from my husband, John, at a more than busy time for us. Thanks, John.

Christmas

It was late December 1788, twelve years after the colonies in America had declared their independence from England, five years after the American Revolution had defeated the might of the British Empire. George Washington was fifty-six and had not yet assumed the presidency of the United States. Thomas Jefferson was forty-five, living in France as our country's minister. The Constitution had not yet been ratified by all thirteen states.

On the western side of the Appalachian Mountains, deep in the wilderness, the snow fell quietly on the hills that surrounded the Ohio River. Hawks and eagles dipped and floated on the air above the water as they patiently waited to spot the fish that would feed their families. Deer stood in compact groups on the shore, grazing in the lush forest that defined the water's edge. The wind blew scattered gusts, its sound blending with the crack of ice floes that rubbed against each other on the swollen and nearly frozen river.

Nature's quiet was broken by the sound of men as they embraced the current and guided crude flatboats through the rushing water, struggling to avoid the ice that could stop their advance. Most of them had come from the other side of the mountains, mainly New Jersey and Pennsylvania. These men were not amateur adventurers. Many of them had been soldiers in the American Revolution. They understood and respected the wilderness. Their flatboats were loaded with necessities they would need: gunpowder, rifles, pistols, glue, needles, seeds, fishing lines, rope, shovels, hoes, flour, whiskey, candles, medicine, salt, potatoes, smoked ham, ink, cutlery, hand tools, blankets, pots, pans, and prayer books. On board there were undoubtedly dogs, a horse or two, and probably pigs.

BEGINNINGS

{ History }

Several of the men in the group had been to the area the previous fall to inspect the land between the Little Miami and the Great Miami Rivers, and they were impressed with the many opportunities it offered for development. They gathered in Limestone (now

twenty-three, carried a box that contained the most important tools on the flatboat. Colonel Israel Ludlow had trained as a surveyor on his father's farm in New Jersey and had already surveyed many important areas. His toolbox contained compasses, a transit, a Wye level, a large

Maysville), Kentucky, and a partnership was formed among Mathias Denman, Colonel Robert Patterson, and Colonel Israel Ludlow. They would form a new settlement in this beautiful area and would spend the next few months in Limestone preparing.

One of the partners, a young good-looking man of

Vernier level, a semi-circumferentor, surveying chains and pins. These tools would make land ready for settlement and determine proper ownership. Colonel Ludlow always knew where his toolbox was.

They left Limestone late on Christmas Eve afternoon. The following day, they probably wished each other

Merry Christmas and then quickly returned to the task at hand. They had to cover sixty-eight miles to reach their objective, eight hundred acres of land beautifully situated across from the mouth of the Licking River in the Ohio country.

They moved carefully through the ice, taking turns at the sweeps, watching for snags in the water, staying on the lookout for danger, be it man or beast, sometimes cursing the raw wet cold that permeated their bodies. On the day after Christmas, the sun appeared briefly and the wind died down a bit. They were making better time than the day before, and when they saw a blockhouse and the small settlement of Columbia that had been formed a few months earlier, they knew they were nearing their destination. They could see people waving and attempted to stop, but the ice prohibited them from reaching the shore. Besides, they knew that they were now only five miles from their goal and they were anxious to press on. Within an hour, they arrived at the spot they had been seeking. Tradition says that they spent that first night in their boats fastened to the roots and shrubs along the shore. The next day they came ashore at a little inlet and proceeded to dismantle their flatboats in order to build a shelter. They spent a busy day unloading supplies, felling trees for firewood, tethering the animals, and creating a shelter. Daniel Drake, a well-known doctor in early Cincinnati, wrote several years later:

Setting their watchman round, they lay down with their feet to the blazing fires, and fell asleep to the music of the north wind whistling among the forest limbs of the great sycamores and water maples which overhung them.

This strong band of men brought with them knowledge of the wilderness, courage, and determination. They also brought the hospitality and cheer that characterize the settlement of Cincinnati to this day. They probably lifted a glass of rum, sang a Christmas carol, and wished each other "Good cheer," delighting in the hope that future generations would do the same.

On December 23, 1959, Herbert Koch, vice president of the Ohio Historical and Philosophical Society, broadcast the following on WLW Radio:

Adventures in America WLW
December 23, 1959 6:37 min.
Cincinnati's First Christmas

Koch: This week, we are celebrating Christmas. On Fountain Square in Cincinnati, two great trees stand as symbols of the Yuletide spirit, and in innumerable homes Christmas trees, holly wreaths, mistletoe, and good cheer hail the happy season.

The abundant tables spread before people in comfortable homes are in marked contrast to the first Christmas celebrated by those who had made their way into this Ohio wilderness and who had come to establish the settlements, which have grown into the great metropolis of Cincinnati.

Columbia, which was to become a part of Cincinnati, on that Christmas day of 1788—one month and seven days after the landing of the settlers—consisted of four blockhouses and fifty settlers. All about them were the forests with Indians that might, or might not, be too friendly; however, for the man that could shoot and was willing to risk his way into the forests, there was an ample supply of game, for the woods held elk, deer, raccoons, squirrels, pheasant, and wild turkeys.

Although on that Christmas day, the river carried a heavy floe of ice, the day was comparatively mild and a feast was laid out on rough tables at the river's edge. A few Indians dropped by and watched curiously. The principal dish was stew, which was cooked in two ten-gallon kettles, and potpie.

This little group had landed at Columbia. What little we know of that first Christmas was given us by Isaac Dunn, who was a small boy when the settlement of Columbia was established in 1788. Many, many years later, in 1857, he wrote a letter to a friend describing the early days.

How about those who settled on the foot of Yeatman's Cove, now Sycamore Street? Actually, they had not yet scrambled ashore. They were not to land and climb up the steep banks until a day or two later. Their Christmas was spent on a flatboat in the middle of the Ohio, surrounded by cakes of floating ice, for that section of the Miami Valley was suffering one of the worst winters it had ever seen. It was on December 24, the day before Christmas, that the brave little band, consisting of some twenty-three men (historians differ as to the exact number), started out from Limestone, now Maysville, Kentucky, to float down the river to that part of the Ohio wilderness that faced the Licking. The band was led by Robert Patterson and their boat was one of those of the "one way" type.

In Marietta, the capital of the great Northwest Territory, the governor, General Arthur St. Clair, issued a Christmas proclamation, for even in this new wilderness, Christmas was to be recognized. The proclamation was given in 1788 in the thirteenth year of the independence of the United States. The hard-bitten governor of the Northwestern Territory wrote: "For as much as it is incumbent on all men to acknowledge with gratitude their infinite obligations to Almighty God for benefits received, and to implore His superintending care and providence for future blessings, I have thought proper to set apart a day for that purpose, and do hereby ordain that Thursday, the 25th day of December, be observed as a day of solemn thanksgiving and praise that the people may, with one voice in sincere thanks, express their grateful sensations… that they may unite in humble supplications to Almighty God that He will be graciously pleased to prosper this infant settlement and the whole territory in their husbandry, trade and manufacturers…and I do hereby prohibit all servile labor on that day."

The Christmas spirit seemed even to have entered the heart of General James Wilkinson. Wilkinson was a severe critic of Anthony Wayne, the "Mad Anthony" who had made such a name for himself during the American Revolution, and who was to recoup the failures of General Harmar and General St. Clair at the Battle of Fallen Timbers. Wilkinson, forgetting, as it has been put, "the acid and bitter side of his nature," sent the following invitation to Wayne as commander-in-chief of the Legion of the United States:

"Major General Anthony Wayne: Mrs. Wilkinson ventures to hope your Excellency may find it convenient and consistent to take dinner with her on the 25th instant with your suite and any eight or ten gentlemen of your cantonment you may think proper to attend you; she begs leave to assure you that dinner shall be a Christmas one, in commemoration of the day and in honor of her guests, and on my part, I will promise a welcome from the heart, a warm fire and a big-bellied bottle of the veritable Lachrymae Christi. We pray you answer.—General James Wilkinson."

Fort Washington, drawn in 1790 by Captain Jonathan Heart, who was killed in the Battle of the Wabash the next year. Published in Charles Cist's *Sketches and Statistics of Cincinnati* in 1851.

ithin one year, the little settlement had grown to eleven families and twenty-four unmarried men. A fort, built to protect the hamlet and the surrounding area, was almost complete. General Josiah Harmar was named to command the fort, and just like the band of men who left Limestone on Christmas Eve the year before, General Harmar left Muskingum on December 24, 1789, and arrived at the fort four days later accompanied by three hundred soldiers. When he arrived, there were probably many shouts of Merry Christmas and good wishes. That was becoming tradition.

With reference to the fort, General Harmar wrote: *"This will be one of the most solid, substantial wooden fortresses, when finished, of any in the Western Territory. It is built of hewn timber, a perfect square, two stories high, with four blockhouses at the angle...The plan is Major Doughty's. On account of its superior excellence, I have thought proper to honor it with the name of Fort Washington."*

Later, Judge Jacob Burnet gave this description of Fort Washington as he remembered seeing it for the first time in 1795:

In Cincinnati, Fort Washington was the most remarkable object. That rude but highly interesting structure stood between Third and Fourth streets, produced east of Eastern Row, now Broadway, which was then a two-pole alley and was the eastern boundary of the town as originally laid out. It was composed of a number of strongly built hewed log cabins, a story-and-a-half high, calculated for soldiers' barracks. Some of them, more conveniently arranged and better finished, were intended for officers' quarters. They were so placed as to form a hollow square of about an acre of ground, with a strong blockhouse at each angle. It was built from large logs cut from the ground on which it stood, which was a tract of fifteen acres reserved by Congress in the law of 1792 for the accommodation of the garrison.

The Artificers Yard was appended to the fort, and stood on the bank of the river, immediately in front. It contained about two acres of ground, enclosed by small contiguous buildings, occupied as workshops and quarters for laborers. Within the enclosure was a large, two-story frame house, familiarly called the "yellow house," which was the most commodious and best finished edifice in Cincinnati. On the north side of Fourth Street, immediately behind the fort, Colonel Sargent, secretary of the Territory, had a convenient frame house and a spacious garden, cultivated with care and taste. On the east side of the fort Dr. Allison, the surgeon-general of the army, had a plain frame dwelling in the center of a large lot, cultivated as a garden and a fruitery, and which was called "Peach Grove."

Fort Washington became the social center of the little village. On Washington's Birthday, February 22, 1791, fireworks and cannon fire preceded the ball held at the fort. Later, when General Wilkinson commanded the fort, he had a large barge built and decorated as a pleasure boat, where he entertained his friends and officers with fireworks and delightful banquets on the river.

Judge Burnet also wrote about social life of the early settlement:

During a large portion of the year, they had to endure fatigues and privations of the wilderness: and as often as they returned from their laborious excursions, they indulged most freely in the delicacies of high living. Scarcely a day passed without a dinner party, the best of wine and other liquors, furnished by the country and by commerce, were served up in great profusion and in fine taste. Genteel strangers who visited the place were generally invited to their houses and their sumptuous tables.

Christmas Balls, dinners, fireworks, and cannon fire appear to have taken place at the fort at Christmastime. After all, it was the birthday of Cincinnati.

The Early Years
1826 – 1850

Cincinnati 1800, from the program for the celebration of Nicholas and Susan Howell Longworth's fiftieth wedding anniversary, Christmas Eve, 1857. From the collection of the Public Library of Cincinnati and Hamilton County.

By 1826, the pioneer village had grown to sixteen thousand people. Cincinnati was thriving. Log cabins had been replaced with frame and brick houses. Now the city had churches, schools, a water system, machine shops, foundries, print shops, a hospital, a medical college, a brewery, banks, even a museum. When steamboats began bringing goods and people to its shores, Cincinnati, recognizing their importance, began building its own steamboats. The city was living up to its title, "The Queen of the West."

Christmas, in these early years, was not a holiday. Folks went to work as usual, perhaps celebrating at the end of the day. Several of the local religious denominations retained various Puritan beliefs and still frowned on Christmas celebrations. Catholics, Episcopalians, and Lutherans, however, kept the tradition and held special observances.

Newspapers of the time give a hint of how the city celebrated the special day. Edward Deering Mansfield, writing in the *Cincinnati Gazette*, December 25, 1869, remembered Christmas, 1826. He was a young man then, living on lower Broadway, and remembers that Christmas Day that year was cold, dry, and beautiful. The river had frozen solid the night before and wagons could be driven across the ice. Some carried the first shipment of Baltimore oysters eagerly awaited by Cincinnatians who had come from the East.

Everyone ate well that Christmas. Prices were low and food was abundant. At the market, an excellent meal could be bought for seventy-five cents and a good one for twenty-five cents. One could find scallops from Massachusetts, terrapin from Maryland, and curried chicken from Illinois. Slaughterhouses would even give away pigs' feet and backbones.

In the *Daily Gazette* of December 24, 1830, an advertisement appeared for a Christmas Eve dancing party at Mrs. Trollope's Bazaar on Third Street. Gentlemen's tickets at $1.50 included refreshments for the ladies.

Gifts were given but not in great numbers. The ads in the *Daily Gazette* of 1830 suggest books or perhaps a length of silk just in from France. If a husband really wanted to surprise his wife, he might come home with one of those new Franklin stoves. He would also get a good piece of mutton to go with the oysters, plum pudding, whiskey, and brandy.

On December 26, 1833, the newspapers reported that a large celebration was held in honor of the forty-fifth anniversary of the landing of the pioneers. The banquet was given at the Commercial Exchange on the riverbank, on the site of the first cabin. The dinner was prepared from foods grown in the region and Nicholas Longworth provided wine from his vineyards in honor of old pioneers and their friends. Among the unusual dishes on the table were roasts of two very large raccoons.

A decade later, Cincinnati had a population of forty-five thousand people. Irish and Germans seeking opportunity in this new land had heard about the lovely city on the Ohio and came in great numbers, bringing with them their talents and gifts. The Germans' contribution was their traditions of Christmas trees and Christmas food. The Irish brought their love of music and the beauty of the written word. Now Cincinnati's Christmas traditions were expanding.

The city, however, did not escape the slavery issue. Opinions on both sides were fiercely debated. In Cincinnati there were many conductors on the Underground Railroad who helped escaping slaves find refuge in this city on the border of slave-holding states. The following extract from the author's *Littsie and the Underground Railroad* brings these issues to life in a scene that takes place on Christmas night, 1834. The narrator, Littsie O'Donnell, has been orphaned by the cholera epidemic of 1832 and is now living with her sister in the barn attached to the home of Harriet Beecher Stowe. Littsie's friend, Euleen Randolph, is a former slave whom Littsie helped escape from slavery. She lives and works at the home of Nicholas Longworth. Both girls are involved with the Underground Railroad.

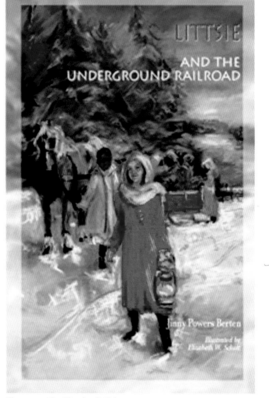

Illustrated by Elizabeth Schott

Littsie and the Undergroud Railroad
Chapter 9 Christmas Reunion

After the Christmas dinner dishes were washed and the kitchen cleaned, I quietly left the house and headed for the barn to get Dan hitched to the sleigh. It was good that he was such a fine work horse, so calm and willing. We asked him to do a lot. The air was turning colder so I put a horse blanket on him and I checked to see if there was one in the sleigh. To my delight, I found that Mr. Perkins had provided a warm buffalo blanket and way in the back seat was a small Christmas tree. That will help, I thought. It will look like we are just celebrating Christmas instead of rescuing enslaved people. I tucked Euleen's present under the blanket and grabbed my scarf, hat, and mittens.

Just as I was about ready to leave, Mina came into the barn. "I was able to get some of the leftovers for you," she said quietly. "You might get hungry. And also I have heated this brick by the fire; it will keep your feet warm in the sleigh." I looked carefully at her. Did she know what I was doing? Did she know about the Underground Railroad? I wasn't sure, but I knew that whoever we were going to find that night might be hungry.

"Thanks," I said, "thanks a lot." Mina smiled and went on back to the house.

As I guided Dan from the house and out onto the road, the snow had turned to flurries and stars were twinkling through the black velvet sky. Silent clouds skidded in view and whispering snowflakes climbed over my face and into my ribboned hair. The forest where we had played in the summer was dressed in brilliant snow that reflected the light of the moon. It was holiday peaceful and as Dan trotted along, I thought of all the people who had helped Megan and me and I was grateful, grateful for Christmas and friends and sisters and books and ribbons and horses and school and snowy nights.

Dan stopped as we came to the ridge overlooking the city as if he wanted to look at the view. At the bottom of the hill lay Cincinnati covered with a blanket of snow. The full moon lit the many church steeples, the houses with smoke curling from their chimneys, and the river beyond. The city shimmered in the snowy moonlight.

"Beautiful, isn't it, Dan?" I said. "But you know we have a lot of work to do tonight. Giddyup, now."

Good old Dan did as I asked and trotted on into the city. As we made our way to the Longworth house to pick up Euleen, you could certainly tell that it was Christmas in Cincinnati. There were candles in every window and wreaths on every door. Folks were gathered in various spots singing Christmas carols and when we passed by the well-lit houses we could see people inside with family and friends enjoying this Christmas night.

Dan took us to the back of the Longworth house, and I quickly got out and knocked on the kitchen door. Euleen answered almost immediately with her hands wrapped around a large bundle.

"Cook says I can have these leftovers," she said. "I think she may know what we are up to. She is a friend of Mr. Casey. Isn't it interesting how many people help in a quiet way with the Underground Railroad?" she asked.

"Yes," I said, "Mina has given us a parcel, too. At least tonight, the folks we help will eat well. Are you ready to go?"

"I am," she said as she put on her coat and scarf and followed me outside.

"Spandy! Littsie, you have a sleigh. How did that happen?"

"Mr. Perkins lent it to Miss Harriet. She said I could use it. It just slides right along. The snow is perfect for it and it makes it easier for Dan."

"And it is fun as well," said Euleen as Dan trotted his way

back to the street. *"Where do we go first?"*

"We have to stop by Mr. Birney's house. He will tell us exactly."

Mr. Birney's home was not far away. When we got there, we could hear singing and we could see people dancing and laughing around the fireplace in the parlor. Euleen knocked softly and in just a few minutes Mr. Birney came to the door.

"Merry Christmas, girls," he said. *"I hope you have been enjoying this jolly day. Are you warm enough? This journey may be a little longer than usual. We hope that four people will be able to cross the river tonight. It is frozen pretty solid and that helps. You are to meet them on the riverbank about two miles from town. Take them on to the Columbia Road. Are you familiar with that road?"*

"Yes, sir," I said, *"I have taken it many times."*

"There is a small house nearby that has an eagle on the weathervane on top of the barn. The folks there said they could help and lead our 'parcel' to the next station. There will be a lantern in the window. The pass word is still 'The Boatman Dance.'"

"Is there anything else we should know?"

"Yes, these slaves have been traveling for a good bit and will probably be cold and hungry. Here, take my coat and my gloves; they may need them. I am glad that you have the sleigh. It will move through the snow a little faster, just in case they are being chased by slave-catchers." Reaching into his pocket, he said, *"They will need at least a little money. Give them this."*

"Thanks, Mr. Birney," I said, *"we will do our best."*

"You girls have done grand work for the Underground Railroad, and the best part is no one suspects you," he said as he tucked the buffalo blanket around us. *"You'd better get going now, the snow has started again and the wind has picked up. Go on ahead, Dan."* Dan lifted his head and with a gentle pull we started for the river. The moon was bright enough to light the way but the snow, coming down so heavily and quickly, made it difficult to see. The reins were getting stiff and difficult to move. I trusted Dan to find the right way.

As we approached the river's edge, I looked for a place that we could hide until we saw the 'parcel' crossing the river. Near the riverbank, I saw an old barn half falling down. It could hide us and also give a bit of shelter. I got off the sleigh and pulled Dan into the small area that was still standing. He was happy to be out of the snow and shook his head in approval. Euleen and I shared the buffalo blanket and kept an eye on the river. The wind was blowing hard now and whistling as it came around the corners of the barn. We could hear the ice on the river cracking and groaning as ice floes hit one another.

"I am glad I don't have to cross that river tonight," I said.

"I would cross anything, in any kind of weather, at any time of night, if it meant that I did not have to be a slave," said Euleen softly. *"Nothing is as bad as being owned by someone else."*

I could only imagine how that would be and I shivered to think of it.

We waited for quite a long time and when we were just

ready to give up we saw a very tiny light in the middle of the river and just the outlines of people.

"Come on," said Euleen, "I think our 'parcel' is here."

We ran in the dark right up to the river and whispered hellos from the shore to the shadows of people. They were crossing the ice with great care, as fast as they could, and looking over their shoulders to see if they were being followed. They had to be aware of everything around them. If they slipped off the ice and into the water, there would be no way that we could help them and it wouldn't take long for the cold water to freeze their bodies. I kept thinking of the story of the lady with the baby that Reverend Rankin told us. Euleen and I tried to be very quiet so that we would not alarm or distract them. We just gave a low whistle so that they would know where we were.

When the group of people finally came to the shore, we could see that it was a man and a woman and two children, a boy and a girl. But that was all we could make out. The man had his hat pulled low to keep out the cold and to hide his face. The woman and the children wore their scarves around their faces and huddled together.

"Follow us," we whispered.

"Do you have a password?" they asked.

"The Boatman Dance," we replied.

"Great God in the morning," the man said. "We made it. We made it to free soil, Celia." And he put his arm around his wife and children and said again, "We made it. We made it."

"Oh, Willis, we did indeed! We did indeed! We all made it safely and we made it together."

"But we must hurry," I said to them. "We need to get you to a safe house just in case there are slave-catchers not far behind. Quickly now, follow us to the barn."

As we led the way through the snow and the wind, I noticed that Euleen was strangely quiet. Most times she would talk to those we helped, explaining all that would happen and telling them where they were and what to expect. But she was silent.

When we got to the barn, I encouraged them to sit down and catch their breath for just a moment. As the man took off his hat I noticed Euleen's face change with astonishment but she remained quiet.

The woman said, "If only Letty were here, then the whole Randolph family would all be together."

Euleen slowly walked toward the woman and took off her scarf to reveal her face and said, "We are all together, Mama."

The woman looked closely at Euleen.

"Is it you, Letty? Is it truly you? Oh Lord, child, I thought I would never see you again. I have cried for you since the day master took you away and sold you. Is it you or am I seeing things?"

"Yes, Mama, it is truly me," said Euleen. "Remember how you gave us a secret name in case we got taken away, a secret name that would identify us so you would know us if we ever found each other? When we met you at the river, I thought there was something familiar in Papa's voice and in the way you walked but I could not let myself believe it. When you said, "If only Letty were here," I knew. That was the secret name you gave me."

With that, there was such jubilation and joy and while the wind howled around the barn the five of them kissed and cried and hugged and hugged some more. Euleen was introduced to the brother and sister she had never met because she was sold before they were born.

"What a Christmas present," she said, "a brother and a sister, Aaron and Betsey."

I was so happy for them all. I was so happy to be part of the Underground Railroad that reunited them and on Christmas at that. When Euleen's papa began to sing with joy, I had to stop him. "Someone could hear you," I said, "and they might not be friendly."

It was Euleen who realized that we had to keep moving and she explained that to her family.

"Hold on, hold on one minute," her papa said. "Could I

give one suggestion? You see that tree in the sleigh. If we tied that to the back of the sleigh, low enough to touch the ground, it would hide our tracks as we went along."

"Yes, yes," I said. "That is a great idea."

We found a piece of rope in the barn and Mr. Randolph tied the tree to the sleigh. It worked perfectly so that you could not see horse or sleigh tracks.

Then the whole group piled into the sleigh and we wrapped the buffalo blanket around everyone and headed out into the snow, the Christmas tree covering our tracks. I tell you, that sleigh was full of so much joy I think it could have flown to the safe house.

This painting by Charles T. Webber depicts the Underground Railroad at work. Three famous Cincinnati abolitionists are portrayed: Catherine White Coffin, far left, her husband, Levi, helping in the wagon, and Hannah Haydock in the center.

Charles T. Webber (American, b.1825, d. 1911), THE UNDERGROUND RAILROAD, The Cincinnati Art Museum 1927.26

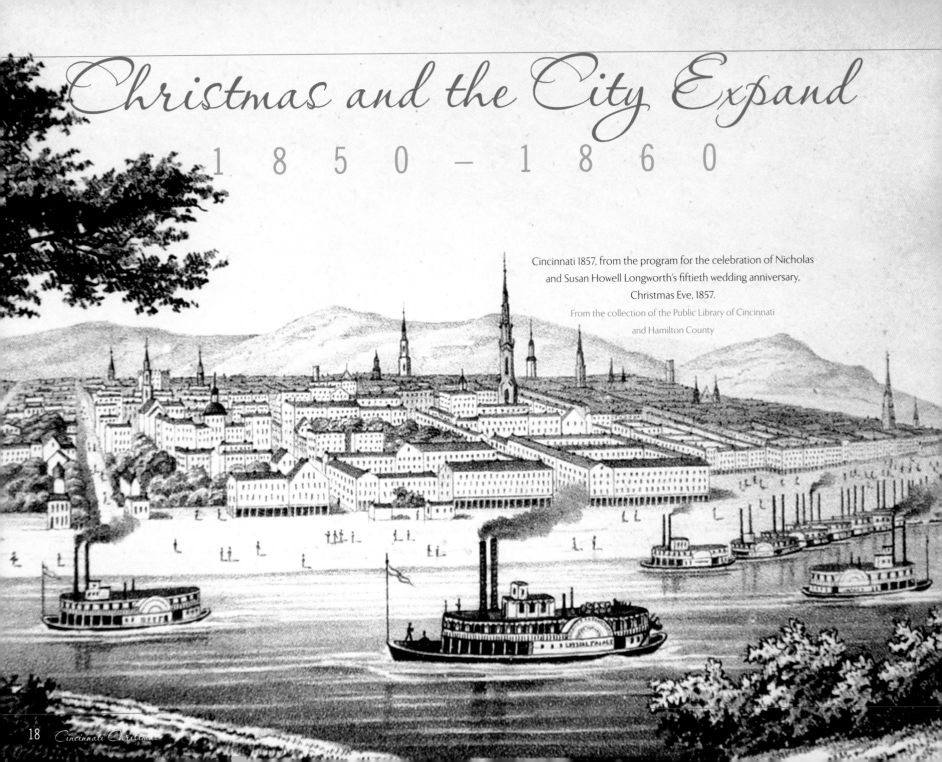

Christmas and the City Expand
1 8 5 0 — 1 8 6 0

Cincinnati 1857, from the program for the celebration of Nicholas
and Susan Howell Longworth's fiftieth wedding anniversary,
Christmas Eve, 1857.
From the collection of the Public Library of Cincinnati
and Hamilton County

By 1850, Cincinnati had a population of 150,000. It had grown over one hundred percent from the population of forty-six thousand ten years before. Sixty-nine thousand people had decided to make their home in the city on the banks of the Ohio River. The city had sixteen thousand buildings, three colleges, four medical schools, a law school, ninety-one churches, four synagogues, Spring Grove Cemetery, an observatory, a fire department, a police department, railroads, steamboats, canals, hotels, bath houses, and libraries. The occupations of its citizens included: 176 attorneys, 287 barbers, 126 brewers, 1,569 boot and shoe makers, 2318 carpenters, 240 engineers, 533 grocers, two fortune-tellers, 298 printers, 23 watchmen, 278 physicians and two dancing masters. Cincinnati was the sixth largest city in the nation. The city was growing and so was Christmas.

The holiday was taking on a different tone. "An Account of a Visit from St. Nicholas" by Clement Moore, first published in 1823, became the familiar poem, "The Night before Christmas" and an American icon. In 1843 Charles Dickens wrote *A Christmas Carol*, adding the great characters of Scrooge, Bob Cratchit, and Tiny Tim to the Christmas celebration.

English author Mary Howitt, best known for her poem "The Spider and the Fly," wrote a little book called *Our Cousins in Ohio*, the chronicle of one year in her sister's life in the Buckeye State. Although she changed names and omitted place names, other details make it plain that her sister was living in or near Cincinnati. The preface to the book says that it is "entirely true." Following is a description of Christmas 1849:

THE Christmas that was just over, had been a very merry one. Instead of roast beef and plum pudding, there had been great roast turkeys and haunches of venison, and mince pies and dough-nuts, and sausages by hundreds of yards, and quails and geese, and candy and cakes, and toys and books, without end.

On Christmas-eve, the children when they went to bed, left their shoes and socks under the sofa. Willie protested that he had no faith in St. Nicholas coming: but as Florence and Nanny believed he would come, he thought he might as well bear their company. In the morning they got up of course long before day-break, but all was empty and silent; and the mother suggested that perhaps, it might be because the shoes were dirty. She had heard, she said, a great crack in the night. Florence immediately thought it must have been Santa Claus running away; more especially as something had scratched her nose in the night. How that might be I cannot tell; but sure enough Florence's dear little nose looked very red, and the little table was seen by day-light standing in a very mysterious manner in the window, covered with a cloth.

When their father came into breakfast, the mother walked across the room, and all at once the cloth was gone from the table, and there was a surprise for the children. There was a large dish of cakes and candy, with mottoes, which their friends in the city had sent for them; and a knife for Willie from his father, and a slate and a pencil; and a silk apron for Florence, from her mother; and a very merry picture book for Nanny and many other things besides.

Santa Claus had indeed been there; nor was little Nellie forgotten. The children counted their treasures over and over again; and then finding that they had so much, they took paper full of cakes and candy to Eberhard for his two little children, and another for Freidrich Lotte, and his little sister, because they wished to make these poor children as happy as they were themselves.

Things happened very remarkably this year. The next morning shoes which had been left overnight, clean and bright without any expectation of reward were found next morning full of kisses. Willie persisted this was his Mother's doing.

One of the most elegant Christmas celebrations in 1857 was the fiftieth wedding anniversary party of Nicholas and Susan Longworth. Nicholas Longworth came to Cincinnati in 1804. He practiced law under Jacob Burnet and began to amass large real estate holdings often accepted as payment for his legal work. By 1830, he had become heavily involved in the making of wine and had over two thousand acres in vineyards.

He was genial, kindly, a mentor to artists, and extremely generous to the poor and to struggling institutions. He had great public spirit, sound judgment, and a deep and abiding love for Cincinnati. He and Susan Howell were married on Christmas Eve in 1807 when Cincinnati was just a small village.

The program for the Longworths' anniversary dinner contains rare and beautiful lithography.

Nicholas and Susan Longworth.
From the collection of the Public Library of Cincinnati and Hamilton County

Lithogr. and Printed by Hunckel & Son, Baltimore.

Left: Program from Nicholas and Susan Howell Longworth's fiftieth-anniversary celebration.

Below: Poem from Longworths' anniversary celebration program.

A merry Christmas Eve is come,
A happy wedding time is here,
And in the old maternal home,
A merry, happy throng appear.
They cluster round the festal board.
With loving heart, in true accord,
To hold an anniversary—
A veritable jubilee:
For, fifty years ago were mated
The twain whence all originated.
In Anno eighteen hundred seven,
The troth of each to each was given:
The parson made them one, I ween
We now may count them seventeen.
Besides some others, grafted fruit,
Not springing from the parent root:
Yet still so admirably paired,

The Civil War and Beyond

CHRISTMAS EVE. '62

Thomas Nast drawings in *Harper's Weekly* gave an accurate portrayal of the mood of the country and the mood of Cincinnati.

1 8 6 0 — 1 9 0 0

When the Civil War began in 1861, people in Cincinnati were saddened and confused. Many had friends and relatives in the South, and Cincinnati had many business connections with Southern companies. However, realizing the threat to the country, the city began forming volunteer brigades, sewing uniforms, and organizing for war. Cincinnati became a center for the care of wounded soldiers and also a center for supplying goods to the Union Army. Cincinnatians produced shoes, clothing, wagons, boats, guns, pontoon bridges, wagons, and iron products. One year, more than 600,000 hogs were shipped to help feed the soldiers. Christmas celebrations took a backseat to these serious activities, but families managed to pack Christmas boxes for their loved ones far away and tried to send them some cheer. Ladies visited a nearby Army camp on Christmas 1863 bringing with them an ambulance full of roast turkeys, mince pies, doughnuts, fruitcakes and apples. The newspapers of the day show that Christmas was still being celebrated. The *Cincinnati Daily Gazette* of December 23, 1863, contained news of the battlefields alongside ads for "Holiday Presents," furs, jewelry and watches and Christmas trees.

Colonel Robert Gould Shaw, who later led the all black 54th Massachusetts Regiment in which several African Americans from Cincinnati served, wrote this letter from Frederick, Maryland, where he was a lieutenant in the 2nd Massachusetts Infantry, at 3:30 a.m., Christmas Day, 1861:

It is Christmas morning and I hope it will be a happy and merry one for you all, though it looks so stormy for our poor country, one can hardly be in a merry humor. My Christmas Eve has been like many other eves during the past six months. It began to snow about midnight, and I supposed no one ever had a better chance of seeing "Santa Claus"; but, as I had my stockings on, he probably thought it not worthwhile to come down to the guard tent. I didn't see any of the guard stockings pinned outside their tent, and indeed it is contrary to army regulations for them to divest themselves of any part of their clothing during the twenty-four hours.

I should like about fifteen more pairs of mittens and some flannel shirts and drawers would be very useful, if there are any spare ones. "Uncle Sam's" are miserable things. "Merry Christmas" and love to all.

"Blue-Eyed Child of Fortune, the Civil War Letters of Robert Gould Shaw" edited by Russell Duncan

When the war ended, there was certainly reason to celebrate, and Christmas became part of that celebration. On New Year's Day in 1867 the Suspension Bridge officially opened. At last Cincinnati had a bridge across its river. Christmas traditions spread and became part of the culture. The custom of having a Christmas tree was becoming common throughout the city. In 1869 little Fanny Taft, sister of President William Howard Taft, was suffering from diphtheria and was confined to her bed. Her brothers, Henry and Horace, tied a Christmas tree to the

ceiling so that she could see it from her bed.

Christmas was finally declared a national holiday by President Grant in 1870. Thomas Nast created the familiar Santa of today: bearded, dressed in a red suit, plump and jolly. Cincinnati adopted that image as well.

Santa and Christmas had been discovered by the downtown department stores. Printed catalogs suggested the perfect gift. Window displays were works of art, enticing customers to come in and shop for their friends.

Charities reminded the public of their needs and requested Christmas donations.

The last three decades of the nineteenth century were full of heady prosperity. In 1880, the city had a population of 250,000. Many of the institutions and landmarks that are treasured today were established during those years: the Cincinnati Art Museum, the Cincinnati Reds, the Cincinnati Zoo and Botanical Gardens, Music Hall, the May Festival, the Cincinnati Conservatory of Music, the Cincinnati Observatory, Tyler Davidson Fountain, Children's Hospital, Rookwood Pottery, the Cincinnati Art Academy, the Cincinnati Symphony Orchestra, Eden Park, Burnet Woods, City Hall, and Hebrew Union College.

Cincinnati was known as "the Paris of America," a city with a fun-loving spirit. It had beer gardens, concert halls, opera houses, theaters, dance halls, and good restaurants. In all these places Christmas was celebrated with hospitality for all.

Above: Shillito's Christmas catalogue, 1878.

Right: Cincinnati Orphan Asylum Christmas appeal, 1876.

CHRISTMAS!
CINCINNATI
ORPHAN  ASYLUM!

REMEMBER THE ORPHANS!

SCENE I.
THE GOOD PEOPLE'S HOUSE.

Enter **Bag** *thin and very Hungry.*
BAG.—"Just popped in, hope I don't intrude?"
GOOD PEOPLE.—"The very poor fellow we were looking for to take a Christmas box!"
Exit **Bag** *as full as he can hold.*

SCENE II.
ORPHAN ASYLUM.

Enter **Bag** *looking quite portly.*
CHILDREN.—"O, welcome **Bag**, and blessings on those who filled and sent you to us!"

MERRY CHRISTMAS TO ALL!
From the Children of the Orphan Asylum
WHO WILL JOYFULLY RECEIVE ANYTHING YOU CAN THINK OF TO EAT, WEAR OR USE.

Faith.

SPLIT PEAS,
TURNIPS,
RAISINS,
HOMINY,
BUTTER,
COFFEE,
TEA,
CAKE,
SUGAR.

GIRLS' CLOTHING,
BOYS' CLOTHING,
WOOLLEN CLOTH,
COTTON CLOTH,
SHOES,
STOCKINGS,
CALICO,
FLANNEL.

Charity.

HOPE.

SPICES,
POTATOES,
HAM,
APPLES,
BEETS,
BEANS,
CHEESE,
RICE,
POULTRY.

SHEETS,
PLATES,
BOWLS,
DISHES,
SPOONS,
KNIVES AND FORKS.
NEEDLES AND THREAD,
COMBS AND BRUSHES,
PINS, ETC., ETC.

Good-Will.

Peace.

GROCERIES,

SEND TO OUR CHRISTMAS TREE.

Handkerchiefs, Nuts, Candy, Scissors, Thimbles, Skates, Sleds, Work Boxes, Slates, Baskets, Hoods, Scarfs, Neckties, Mittens, Gloves, Hair Ribbons, Lead Pencils, Drawing Paper, Color Boxes, Evening Games, Dominoes, Backgammon, Games of Authors, Games of History, and whatever else you please.

Send this Bag on or before Dec. 23rd to any of the following Managers.

Mrs. CATHERINE BATES, Walnut Hills.
" JOHN D. JONES, Glendale.
" ELIZA J. FUNK, 94 West Eighth Street.
" HENRY PROBASCO, Clifton.
" AARON F. PERRY, Mt. Auburn.
" S. M. HINSDALE, 394 West Seventh Street.
" JOHN DAVIS, 325 Elm Street.
" S. J. BROADWELL, 66 Lawrence Street.
" A. D. BULLOCK, Mt. Auburn.
" J. H. CHEEVER, Mt. Auburn.

Mrs. G. H. BARBOUR, 90 East Fourth Street.
" JOHN R. WRIGHT, Walnut Hills.
" A. S. WINSLOW, Corner Broadway and Fourth St.
" WILLIAM JUDKINS, Cor. Race and Center Sts.
" M. F. FORCE, 89 West Eighth Street.
" L. E. YORKE, Clifton.
" C. T. H. STILLE, 85 Broadway.
Miss JANET C. BROWN, 135 West Seventh Street.
PROCTOR & GAMBLE, No. 20 West Second Street.
BARBOUR, STEDMAN & HEROD, 77 West Pearl St.

Or to the CINCINNATI ORPHAN ASYLUM, Mt. Auburn.

Fountain Square Pantomime was painted by Cincinnati artist Joseph Henry Sharp in 1892.

Cincinnati Art Museum. Gift of the CAM Docent Organization in celebration of its fortieth anniversary and The Edwin and Virginia Irwin Memorial. 2000.68.

Square

In order to lure customers to their establishments, some stores put on small holiday plays. Mabley & Carew presented pantomimes on a large glass-covered balcony facing Fountain Square. In an age before radio, TV, text messaging, or video games, this was the biggest show in town. Most children came at least once. On Christmas Eve, Mabley & Carew gave a box of candy to every child who came to the store. What a treat!

In 1892, local artist Joseph Henry Sharp painted a picture of children watching the pantomime. For many years, it was displayed on the third floor of the store; currently it hangs in the Cincinnati Wing of the Cincinnati Art Museum.

☆ 1941

"Christmas Eve 1890, Cincinnati—Drawn up on the Ivorydale siding were carloads of squawking turkeys waiting for the factory signal to announce the holiday shutdown. The small red switch engine, The Ivorydale, had been traveling busily over the mile and a half of track, which connected the rail lines bounding the Ivorydale plant. Just as it did each year on the day before Christmas, The Ivorydale had made its traditional run to the main line to pick up two freight cars of live turkeys. Those turkeys were the company's Christmas gifts to employees.

Upon leaving the plant, each employee was asked to select one of the bright-eyed birds. The turkey was then hauled from the railcar, grabbed by the legs, and desperately held on to; flapping its wings wildly, the turkey was no easy match. When a bird got loose, everyone joined in the chase to return it to its owner, but it's said that some pursued their Christmas dinner all the way home.

Such excitement prevailed for twenty years, until in 1910 a dressed turkey was substituted for the live model. By 1920 the turkey had become only a fondly recalled memory as the company adopted a seasonal basket filled with a variety of staples. Only employees living in a household received a basket in the early days, however. Cartons of cigarettes or boxes of candy were given to single people who boarded.

Over the years the basket has taken many forms—a wicker basket, Skotch Kooler, a wooden pail, a traveling bag.

In late November, suppliers began shipping the baskets and

their ingredients by truck and rail to P&G locations across the United States. Company employees assembled the gifts.

On that 1890 Christmas Eve about six hundred turkeys were distributed. This year (1974) 170,000 pounds of ham were purchased to provide personal gifts to all P&G employees.

The basket would not be complete without the traditional company card.

Every year since 1837, sending Yuletide greetings to P&G families has been a Procter and Gamble custom. At first, these greetings could be extended personally.

As the company grew, this became impossible and since 1924, a printed card has been sent from the company to each employee. Illustrated by a well-known artist, the card usually depicts some interesting aspect of P&G.

In 1929, the cards began to illustrate some incident in P&G history. The first told "the story of Christmas 1937."

Regardless of the year, the card design, or the form the basket takes, one thought has remained constant since 1937—the warm wish that P&G families everywhere have a merry holiday season and a prosperous new year.

In 1924, the message of the first company card from William Cooper Procter, then president of Procter and Gamble read: "The very thought of Christmas calls forth the spirit of service to others.

'Shall we not make this spirit endure throughout the coming year by trying to appreciate each other's problems, and by working together make our company more closely knit through mutual affection and respect? With such a spirit of service we will attain still greater heights: without it our future will be limited, as no false standard can succeed, just as truly no high standard can fail.

'May Christmas this year bring to all of us this spirit of service and affection.'

Illustrated are two Procter and Gamble cards; one recalls the turkey distribution (previous page) and the other the Procters and the Gambles visiting each other on Christmas day."

Excerpted from an article in the 1974 issue of The Procter & Gamble Company Magazine, Moonbeams. Used with permission of the P&G Corporate Archives.

Christmas Greeting
1939

rthur M. Hopkins (1865–1935) was a Cincinnati journalist and banker. He often sent Christmas letters to his friends all over the world. In 1925 he wrote the following letter recalling life fifty years before. He brings to life the world of 1875 and the spirit of Christmas past.

A Christmas Letter
by A. M. Hopkins
Cincinnati, December 20, 1925

My Dear Friend:

How could I permit the blessed Christmas season to pass without writing to you? I'm seated in a big chair, alone with my memories. A log is smoldering in the grate. I smell wood smoke. The wind sings plaintive songs in the chimney. From away off somewhere the whistle of a locomotive sounds like a cry of distress. The scenes that come to me are not mine alone. They belong to most men and women who have passed the fiftieth milestone, and so I write my greeting from the heart and feel sure that in some mysterious way I have sent a hand clasp over the miles and around the world to make those who have given me their love and friendship know that they are dear to me. I suppose that in millions and more millions of homes preparations for Christmas are in progress, and human love is reaching its crest. He who makes a child happy deserves well of God.

We are getting on, getting on surely, and so we speak often of what we have done and less of our plans. Grey hairs are ours, but, thank the Almighty, in our hearts flaming youth abides.

Will you go back with me fifty years and study the pictures in the firelight? There is the old home in the country, with its privations and its comforts. There is the little room where we slept under the eaves; where we took flat-irons to bed to warm our feet and where we heard the floor boards snap with the cold, in the night. We removed our boots in the kitchen and placed them by the stove to dry.

Do you remember the stove, with its raised letters. Read them now: "STEWART'S SUMMER AND WINTER AIR TIGHT COOKING AND HEATING STOVE." I learned most of my letters on that kitchen comfort that burned hard maple wood and that was the center of our household economy. We lived in the kitchen, for this was before the age of invention. We lived as most of our neighbors did, simply as became our poverty, for little of wealth had ever come our way.

There's the table over by the south wall, with the old clock ticking away on the mantel. It limped for half a century and once father took it to the pump and pumped water through it for ten minutes to subdue its irregularities. He was a great musician, a genius, but he didn't know much about clocks.

Six children at the table, with mother behind the coffee pot and father asking the blessing. Are there people who are asking blessings in these swift-moving days? Hear him with his head bowed: "We thank Thee, Dear Lord, for the food that Thou hast set before us. May it give us strength to do Thy will. Forgive us

our trespasses and grant that we may so live as to inherit the Kingdom of Heaven. For Christ's sake, Amen."

And after breakfast mother read a chapter in the Bible and we sang

"Come ye disconsolate, where e'er ye wander;

"Come to the Mercy seat,—"

Ah! I have forgotten the words, but I still hear mother's trembling soprano and father's rich baritone.

My memory finds romance in the chores that must be done. The chickens were fed, the angular cow, she who meant so much to us in the matter of living, was milked, the stable was cleaned, and then we plunged into the drifts and shoveled paths. The merry jingle of sleighbells told that some farmer was passing on his way to the cheese factory, for in those days, cheese was made in Ohio.

Not one modern invention about the place, and we had never even seen a dining car, a sleeping car, a daily newspaper, or slept one night outside of our own home. From movies down to frozen suckers, we went without, and it was good for us. I wonder if modern life would not do better with the developing force of personal hardship.

I also wonder what the modern lad would do if he had to fight a snowstorm, to obtain stove wood from a frozen pile, beating the ice from each stick, struggling for breath as he bore his burden to the ever yawning woodbox back of the kitchen stove.

And yet there was a great deal of happiness in that little home with its oil lamps and even candles; its rag carpets; its homemade almost everything. It was a happy home, and tonight I wish I might go back to the hours around the evening lamp, with mother reading Little Women aloud, and her children not only listening but living the story that has been so beautifully told.

Do other men in the sixties realize what mothers of that other day did and bore and endured, all with a smile? God certainly sets his approving mark on such women. They are the handmaidens, the wives, the mothers, the comforters, the refuge, the advisers and it is meet that their children should rise up and call them blessed.

Grandmother Andrews gave to the world thirteen sons and daughters and never had a "hired girl," as we once called them. She lived to see 84 years, and I never saw her idle. She knitted miles of stockings and mittens and wristlets, and somewhere in Heaven, if such a thing be possible, she is knitting now—perhaps sunbeams into halos. Who knows? And as she lived so did my mother and millions of other mothers. They cooked, washed, mended, swept, dusted, and even made clothes for the brood. And never a complaint and always a smile. God gave them stout hearts.

I was twelve years old when I wore my first overcoat, and very proud, too. It was made out of father's old one, and mother sewed a bit of fur above the pockets, a mark of aristocracy. Later, the next brother grew into it. Nothing was wasted that could be used, and father's greatest possession outside of his beloved violin was his Sunday suit of black broadcloth that gathered lint at *every step and was as sable as the dark of midnight.*

And again I am sitting through my first show, done in the Little Church with the Cracked Bell, for so it was known, and the footlights were oil lamps, and Clarence Parmelee played the leading part in The Persecuted Dutchman, and "Cory" Alvord was the most wonderful of hoboes. I'll never laugh so much again because I will never have the peculiar sense of humor that was mine as a lad. And the Hopkins family made up the orchestra, and as the times were, it was a good orchestra. Father played with not one hint of jazz, for jazz music and jazz living were still far over the horizon. It matters not that the chief instrument was a four-octave melodeon, for father made it peal out harmony. What an evening! In every detail it stands before me, after fifty years.

School? A mile away, and through snow drifts, for we had winters Back Yonder, and there is the first time that I found the courage to ask a girl for anything. Her name was Sallie Patterson and she looked to me like an angel. I invited her to slide down hill on my sled and Romance was mine until we went over a bump, there was a scream and a flourish of legs clad in red stockings, and I slunk away like beaten dog, with my eyes filled with tears. Why try to be a man, at all?

Christmas. July 4. Decoration Day. The last day of School. The day our copy of The Youth's Companion arrived.

Those were the five big dates on the calendar, and Christmas, with its mystery, its joy, its happiness that can never be measured, stood at the head of the list. I like to think that as life changes, a never ending procession of new faces and new times and ideas, that human love, toleration, consideration, tenderness, sympathy, are just as God made them in the beginning. We love as we did a century ago; and the good in us; all the elements that make for human uplift, were a part of the divine and immortal spark in the beginning. It must be so. The world could not live if there could be anything to take the place of a mother's love, or of human kindness, no matter what form it takes.

Tonight I would like to light a candle and go exploring in the dark cellar. I would fill a basin with russet apples, and the largest one that could be found would be for mother, and on the way up the cellar stairs I would rub a bit of polish on its rough skin with my coat sleeve. And she would say: "What! The biggest for me? What a boy you are!" And she would run her dear fingers through my hair and there would be a kiss from lips that trembled so easily.

The clock does not turn backward. We are getting on—getting on,—and we'll try to wear our grey locks with dignity and face life unafraid, as becomes the sons and daughters of our fathers and mothers.

Merry Christmas, and with it, Good night and God bless you.

Courtesy Cincinnati Museum/Cincinnati Historical Society Library

vatory 1873

Twentieth Century Christmas

1 9 0 0 — 1 9 9 9

The next hundred years were to bring profound and lasting changes to the river city. Inventions that had only been dreamed of would dramatically alter life in Cincinnati: streetcars, telephones, airplanes, cars, radio, television, movies, washing machines, dryers, indoor plumbing, electricity, transistors, computers, jet engines, and space travel.

The century, the country, and Cincinnati would experience five wars: World War I, World War II, the Korean War, Vietnam, and the Gulf War. In spite of all this, there was still Christmas, still a day that celebrated peace, generosity, and goodwill for all.

In 1978 Lew Moores, of the *Cincinnati Post*, wrote the following article imagining what it might have been like in Cincinnati on Christmas 1901.

Vignettes of Cincinnati's 1901 Christmas
By Lew Moores
Post staff reporter

The following story is the product of imagination and fact. All of the incidents are real—gleaned from the pages of newspapers and Frederick Lewis Allen's *The Big Change*—though some have been embellished. The setting is Cincinnati at the turn of the century, December 25, 1901. It is the first Christmas of the new century.

THEY FOUND Joe Atkins and his wife and child of four years over in the coal yard on West Sixth Street. The thermometer was holding around zero and small piles of coal held fast against the shovel. Joe and his family lived in a tin-patched hut in the yard. Rolled newspaper was stuffed in the cracks in the walls.

An agent of Associated Charities found the family. Joe and his wife welcomed the visitor with holiday cheer, though their teeth clattered uncontrollably. Joe's daughter saluted the agent, her hand concealed by a mitten.

Many of us know Joe Atkins. At least we know who he is. He's a quiet sort, never asked for anything. He peddles coal from a rickety old wheelbarrow and does odd jobs around town. Just before Thanksgiving, his other child, an infant, died. The baby was buried in Wesleyan Cemetery. There were only two mourners, Joe and his wife.

The agent talked the family into going with him, to Vine Street for Christmas dinner.

We never knew where Joe Atkins lived before.

SANTA CLAUS was generous to Wall Street today, this the first Christmas of the new century. Gods of Finance smiled from blue heavens. The magnates were full of Christmas cheer.

Andrew Carnegie's personal income has already exceeded the $23 million he made last year. The principal clerks in J.P. Morgan's Wall Street office each received a crisp $5,000 gold certificate. Everyone else, including the office boys, obtained half their yearly salaries as Christmas bonuses. Morgan's gifts totaled $140,000.

At William K. Vanderbilt's palatial Idle Hour on Long Is-

land, holiday guests began arriving in the morning. Later in the day, the diners would sit down in one of the home's 110 rooms and enjoy a Christmas feast of small Blue Point oysters, wild turkey roasted golden, saddle and rack of lamb, cranberry, fresh fruit, hard cheese, Brussel sprouts sauté, new asparagus with cream sauce and vinaigrette; the feast welcomed with sherry, accompanied by wine and concluded with cognac.

CHRISTMAS BROKE cold today, but the promise of the new century will not be found in gray skies. It can be found in our mills and factories, in our prosperity, in our scientific achievements, in the penumbra of hearths snapping with burning logs, in the radiance of evergreens festooned with ribbon and yellow candies. Tis the season to redeem the promise…

Argentina and Chile are talking war. There is sharp fighting in the Orange River and Transvaal colonies of South Africa, there are reports of an imminent uprising in Cuba. In the Philippines, our American Army is becoming increasingly expensive to keep there, due partly to the activity of insurgents on the Island of Samar, in Batangas and Tayabas provinces and other places.

Here in America, the average working day lasts 10 hours; the work week, six days. Annual earnings average $400 to $500. In the garment district in New York, the ladies are working 70 hours a week and 26 percent of all boys in America between the ages of 10 and 15 are gainfully employed.

From St. Johns, Newfoundland, Marconi sends a message to the Wizard of Menlo Park, Thomas Edison: "Thanks for your very kind letter to the press. I hope soon to show you wireless telegraphy working between the United States and Europe. I wish you a happy Christmas."

There is the promise of lesser achievement. Two Californians arrived in Chicago two days ago to build a plant for the manufacture of an automatic fly trap. It will catch flies at the rate of a million every minute. The trap acts like a turnstile. A circular disk of tin is made to revolve. Flies congregate on the portion of the disk that is baited with beer or sugar. The disk rotates, carrying its victims to a cage that rests on the other half of the disk. There is no escape.

And, of course, there is Ivory Soap. It floats.

Yesterday there were 2,000 people skating on frozen sheets of ice at Lincoln Park, the Burnet Woods lake, the Zoo lake, Taylor Bottoms, Ludlow Lagoon and some canal basins. There were cheers and merriment. The parks were a sea of brightly colored scarves, children bundled to their eyes like living holiday packages.

At the foot of Columbia Street in Newport, the Rev. C.P.M. Bigbee, pastor of the first Baptist Church, walked into the icy Ohio to his waist and received six converts one by one. Several hundred people stood at river's edge and watched. The six emerged from the river, shoulders twitching, but all six are reported in good health and spirits today. Mr. Bigbee, however, contracted a severe cold and was unable to speak today.

The Salvation Army has been out in force on downtown streets the past few days, standing by their pots, capturing attention with their bells. They are noisy soldiers who say very little and mean very much.

On Sixth Street, a florist told us the mistletoe trade is gradually dying. "Perhaps the young men of today are not as daring as the old," the florist told us, "or maybe the maidens are too timid to venture under it. I don't know, but I think its loss of popularity is due to the innate propriety of the American people. Indiscriminate kissing is repulsive to the gentle-born."

Detective Jack Cainan, an old friend and inveterate tipster, stopped us on Seventh Street and told us about Cornelius Van Hof-fen of Cleveland who went into Mabley & Carew Monday and purchased more than $200 worth of merchandise with a bad check. Cainan puffed with pride as he told us how he tracked the transgressor down at a downtown hotel. "That's C-a-i-n-a-n," the detective said, hitching his pants and patting the revolver under his overcoat.

While checking the parks a few days before Christmas for sledders and ice skaters, we paid a visit to Prof. Jermaine G. Porter at the University Observatory in Mt. Lookout near Ault Park. Prof. Porter is an astronomer at the University of Cincinnati, though, of course, he spends a good deal of his time with his eye on the heavens.

We asked the professor about wireless telegraphy and communications with other worlds. "The moon seems to be as barren as a snowball," the professor began, "with frozen mountain chains and waterless oceans. It was long ago depopulated of people, if any ever existed there."

"And Mars?" we asked.

"The thermometer there likely registered 150 degrees below zero," he said. "If beings exist, they are of a vastly different makeup from the people of Earth. It is generally accepted by astronomers that Mars is not habitable.

"I indicate Venus as the most hopeful planet for experimenting with Marconi's wireless telegraphy, because it more nearly resembles the Earth in its physical conditions. So far as Jupiter and Saturn go, the temperature of those planets is probably very high. The habitability of those planets is out of the question, except possibly by a race of Salamanders."

THE SILENCE of a Sabbath hung over Cincinnati Christmas Day. It was cold and gray. Stores, offices and factories were closed. The streets were virtually clear of pedestrians and traffic; only churches claimed attendance. Those who left the churches after services said, "Keep the change," to newsboys and street car conductors.

The Salvation Army distributed 350 baskets of food to the needy from a storefront at 510 Vine Street. Each basket contained a chicken, potatoes, canned tomatoes and corn, turnips, cabbage, celery, a loaf of bread, beans, coffee and sugar. One woman, 70 years old, wrapped in a heavy overcoat with a coarse brown scarf that hid her face, walked from Findlay Street for her basket.

At the House of Refuge, superintendent Allison brought delight to the faces of 500 children when he had St. Nick come down a real chimney, in spite of the fact that many of the children yelled, "Hi, Mr. Allison!" when Santa emerged from the fireplace. At the courthouse, clerks in the auditor's office each received a turquoise stickpin, and sheriff's deputies each received a turkey.

The old and sick inmates at the City Infirmary sat down to a Christmas dinner of soup, celery, pork and beans, turnips, potatoes, mince pie and tea. Superintendent Michael Heister brought in 17 turkeys in the morning, but they were handed out to infirmary employees.

We asked Heister whether this was a queer way of saying, "Peace on Earth, Goodwill to All."

"Nearly all the inmates are old and they say they prefer pork and beans," Heister told us. "The vote was 10-to-1 for pork and beans."

We asked the superintendent whether we could speak with any of the inmates alone. Reluctantly, he agreed. "We took the vote yesterday," he called after us. "I don't know what they might say today."

We came upon one old man standing by his bed, wearing a robe. "It's absurd to say we'd rather have pork and beans than turkey," he said. "We may be old and penniless, but we're not completely foolish." We spoke with close to a dozen inmates, and all but one preferred turkey. The exception was a rather frail, toothless man with spots on his hands. He told us he thought pork would be easier for him to chew.

"So they changed their minds," Heister barked. "They should've changed them yesterday when we took the vote."

The Pen and Pencil Club was formed by a group of Cincinnati journalists around 1900. Each year they published a calendar and almanac. The following Christmas story appeared in the publication of 1909.

How I played Santa
by Roe S. Eastman

It was a very unseasonable Christmas Eve. Thermometers registered about 60 degrees; sickly blasts of warm air sailed lazily about the tops of tall buildings and fell uncomfortably upon thousands of beaded brows in the streets below; a drizzling rain, which had set in early in the afternoon, completed the prevailing atmosphere of discomfort and ill humor.

In sore need of sleep, I left the office at a late hour, and by sheer force of will wedged my body into the congealed mass of humanity upon the rear platform of a suburban car. My precarious though highly scientific performance of balancing upon three-sixteenths of the lower step, with the aid of two fingernails hooked into the coat-tail of a more fortunate passenger, was brought to a delightful end when the car reached my destination. Once more finding myself upon terra firma, I gazed after the departing car, bulging with Christmas shoppers and their booty, and while I stretched the kinks out of my cramped muscles said a few uncomplimentary things about the traction company and the idiocy of those who maintained the ancient Christmas customs.

Then I started for home and bed. A row of two-story red bricks, all owned by the same landlord, built by the same contractor from the same plan and material, stretched on one side of the block as far as I could see. I paid for board and lodging at the sixth door from the corner. It was not necessary for me to count the doorways, however. I had walked from the car to the house and from the house to the car so often that my feet naturally turned in at No. 12, just as the old plow horse will unerringly find his stall at night. As usual, I had considerable trouble with the latch, but the door finally yielded and I hurried upstairs to my room.

When I turned on the light a most peculiar object confronted me. There, suspended from my mantel, was a large, pink stocking, the nether finery of a very large, fancy woman. In the depths of this elaborate receptacle I could discern the outlines of a number of bulky packages. Doubtless this was somebody's misconception of a clever joke upon the habitual victim of the household. With a cynical smile I picked up a lump of coal and said aloud: "Well, I'll contribute a black diamond to the little lady's Christmas, anyhow."

Just as I was about to drop the coal into the stocking I was interrupted by a drowsy female voice emanating from a far corner of the room.

"W-what?" it questioned, in a half-startled tone. There could be no mistake. A sudden realization of my predicament flashed upon my now frightened senses. The chunk of coal made a loud clatter on the hearth and I made a dash for the one window across the room. Without a doubt I would have jumped to my death, taking glass and sash with me, had not a whirling chrysalis of blankets and bed comforts pounced upon me, and with a piercing shriek pinioned me to the floor under a weight that seemed nothing less than that of an elephant or an upright piano. From within this mass of bedclothes hysterically reposing upon my chest, two short, fat arms encircled my neck with the grip of an octopus while a volley of screams that would have done credit to any revival meeting was poured into my already deafened ears.

It did not last long, thank heaven, and when that mountainous bulk was lifted off me I almost welcomed the lusty kick in the ribs and the stunning blows of the jaw as I was jerked to my feet to confront the six feet of indignant manhood compris-

ing the young woman's irate brother.

With incredible rapidity the cry of burglars was echoed through the neighborhood, and soon the house was filled with curious though well-minded busybodies. My attempt to explain was, of course, wasted upon two husky policemen who came post-haste at the first alarm.

"You're a foine Sandy Claus," exclaimed one of them as he attached me to a pair of cold handcuffs. "An' where the divil is yer pack of prisints an' toys?"

Finally, just as I was being led to the patrol box, Mrs. Digby waddled in and the good old lady in a perplexed and rather incoherent manner managed to explain that I was her boarder at No. 12, who, in some (to her inexplicable) manner had stumbled into the house next door by mistake. After a series of jesting apologies had been made by members of the family upon whose privacy I had so innocently intruded, I was taken home safely. Well, it is all over now and I have moved into a house with a bay window, the only one on the block, so I can't miss it. Still, every now and then the stern vision of the lonely cell at Central in which I so narrowly missed lodging for one dreary Christmas looms up before me and a cold shiver plays leap-frog over the notches of my backbone.

Courtesy Cincinnati and Hamilton County Public Library

The years before World War I are remembered as the mellow years. Cincinnati now had a reputation as being the "wettest" city between New York and Chicago. Vine Street had fancy bars and not so fancy ones. Some even gave a free bratwurst with every drink. At Christmas they sang "O Tannenbaum" in the German bars and "Galway Bay" in the Irish bars. This was a jolly city.

In 1911, E. T. Hurley created a work that captures the essence of Cincinnati Christmas. *The Midnight Mass* portrays Immaculata Church at midnight on Christmas Eve. The Roman Catholic church atop Mount Adams can be seen from all over Cincinnati. At the time of this painting, German immigrants lived on one side of Mount Adams and Irish immigrants lived on the other side. Hurley worked as an artist for the Rookwood Pottery, which was also in Mount Adams.

The mellow years did not last long. By 1917, the country was once again at war and once again Cincinnatians did their part. Cincinnati workers built rifle bores, shell casings, motors, camp stoves, cooking equipment, clothing, foodstuffs, drugs, and shoes. Twenty-five thousand of our young men went off to war; many would never return. And still, Christmas and its celebration remained. Boxes full of gifts were sent to the soldiers overseas and a fund was created to help fatherless children in France.

Within a few years of the return of our young men, prohibition legislation was passed and "the wettest city" became bone dry. The bars were closed and to give a Christmas toast a bootlegger had to be found. Cincinnati had many of those.

In those postwar years, Cincinnati grew and expanded.

By 1930, the population had increased to 451,000. The tallest building in the city, the Carew Tower, now took its place in the city skyline. WLW and the Opera at the Zoo lent renown to the city. The Great Depression and the flood of 1937 brought tragedy to the area, and yet there was still Christmas. In 1924, the first municipal Christmas tree was erected on Fountain Square and there has been one there ever since. Folks still shopped downtown, enjoyed the Christmas windows, and saw Laurel and Hardy in *Babes in Toyland* at the Albee theater that had opened on Christmas Eve in 1927. They could also wander into the Netherland Plaza in the Carew Tower to see the city's largest indoor decoration. The Christmas tree in the lobby held five hundred lights and ten thousand ornaments. It was a spectacular sight for the hotel guests, the people who came to the dances in the Hall of Mirrors, and the downtown shoppers.

The Midnight Mass (1911) by E. T. Hurley.
Cincinnati Art Museum. Gift of Mr. and Mrs. Simon Hubig. 1911.1372.

Procter & Gamble employees with their Christmas baskets, circa 1920.

rocter & Gamble employees no longer had to struggle with a live turkey to get it home. Now the company gave over six thousand boxes, each filled with a twelve-pound ham, candy, nuts, and cigarettes.

In 1939, the Western and Southern Life Insurance Company erected a stable in Lytle Park to commemorate the first Christmas. Thousands of people visited it. In the same year, Ruth Lyons, a pioneer radio and TV broadcaster, established a Christmas Fund for patients at Children's Hospital. The fund provided toys, games, and programs to comfort hospitalized children. To date, the fund has generated over $20 million.

The same year, 1939, a new tradition was added, scheduled to take place twelve days after Christmas, sometimes known as Twelfth Night. The Southwestern Chapter, Thirty-Seventh Division, A.E.F. Veterans Association organized a huge bonfire for that night in memory of a distant battlefield and of the men who were with them. The bonfire was built with spent and unsold Christmas trees, two thousand of them. They were gathered at Jackson Hill Park in Mount Auburn, chosen because at one time it was known as Bethlehem Hill and the bonfire there could be seen from all over the city.

The trees were doused with twenty gallons of kerosene. Once lit, the flames grew to over fifty feet and lasted several hours. Vigilant firemen stood by and kept a watchful eye. Crowds gathered to sing a last Christmas carol, remember the Feast of the Epiphany, and say goodbye to the Christmas season.

The first week of December 1941, downtown Cincinnati was ready for the holiday season. The tree was up on Fountain Square, window displays were ready, and department stores were decorated, but by Sunday, December 7, things had changed drastically. The bombing of Pearl Harbor sent the country quickly into war, and that would affect Christmas for the next four years.

The country needed everything to fight the war. The toys children wished for the year before were no longer available:

no trains, bikes, or BB guns, nothing made of metal. Santa now had to bring wooden toys. Mother had to save her ration stamps so that there could be at least a little Christmas feast. Even lights for the Christmas tree were unavailable.

Because of meat rationing, Procter & Gamble could not give its employees their normal Christmas gift of a lovely ham. Instead, they gave their workers a crisp five-dollar bill in an envelope that portrayed pigs going off to war.

A portion of your Christmas cheer,

Must be a money gift this year,

Because your favorite Christmas ham

Is proudly serving Uncle Sam!

Procter & Gamble

Left and above: Images used with permission of the P&G Corporate Archives

A Christmas bonfire was set on what was once known as Bethlehem Hill in Mount Auburn, in celebration of the ending of the Christmas season.

Soldier opening Christmas package from his wife while his buddies share the treats, 1944.

There was still singing on Fountain Square, but folks sang with heavy hearts as they thought about the boys fighting all over the world. They packed Christmas boxes for their boys so that wherever they were, they would know they were not forgotten.

And the boys wrote home. PFC Ralph C. Lewis, Jr., inducted at Fort Thomas, Kentucky, in 1942, sent the following to his parents from "somewhere in Africa" in 1943:

Africa, 1943

Due to all my holiday activities I haven't written a line to anyone since the first of the month but I just couldn't let Christmas Day pass by without at least a short note to wish you both the very best of the season and join with you in the prayer that we may all be united once more to celebrate next Christmas in a peaceful world. My thoughts are with you and the old homestead today more so than on any other day and in my heart I'm so very lonely and blue on this the happiest of days. Sure, I admit I'm homesick and lonesome but what soldier isn't who is thousands of miles from his loved ones in a strange land? Doubtless both of you feel the same way but all of us can find cheer in the fact that we can share our thoughts and prayers and that all of us are enjoying the best of health this Christmas Day. When compared to those families whose sons will never return then our own family has been singularly fortunate and I thank God that I still enjoy the best of health despite my better than two years on foreign soil.

We have erected a small tree in our camp and decorated it with a few small ornaments and wrappings from Christmas packages. Not much of a Christmas tree it's true but to those of us that haven't seen a tree since 1941 it's quite a novelty! The last two years on Christmas we were much too busy to bother much about Christmas but this year we can afford to relax a wee bit and permit ourselves a little treat. Funny thing but I appreciate that little tree and the Xmas packages I've received thus far much more than I did all the expensive toys and gifts I got when I was a kid. I suppose it takes something like a war to wake some of us selfish lads up and make them realize what an eternal debt they owe to parents like you two. So, though I'm many miles from home this Christmas Day, I send you all my love and my deepest wish for a very merry Christmas.

I find it hard to realize that I will be "somewhere over here" for another Christmas. I know last year scarcely seemed like Christmas and this year will no doubt be much the same. As Irving Berlin put it in his song last year, "I'm dreaming of a white Christmas—just like the ones I used to know, etc." How he has captured the feelings of this soldier in that song! And how fitting for one far far away in a land that has never known snow! Yes, I suppose that I and many others dream a lot of those happy Christmases before the war with the Xmas trees and laughter and all the joyfulness of the season. But the Xmas cards and packages that you and Dad and the family send go a long long way towards making Christmas a little less lonely and sad for me. And it's the same with the other boys, too. Who cares what's

in the packages? It's just the idea that the package itself serves to give the soldier a little Christmas of his own and helps to ease the longing and homesickness in his own heart. On that day as on no other—the boys turn their thoughts toward home and their loved ones and picture those happy Christmases of yesterday with the snow and all—and hope that ere long "Peace on earth and goodwill to man" will once again be restored to the world. And it is surprising how much we appreciate even the most insignificant things (or at least I do now!) Things like the snow—the green grass and rolling hills and trees back home—the birds—and such things that I never noticed before now have a new meaning for me. So, though war is terrible and harbors many tragedies—it can still teach people to appreciate what they have. While other boys may not see it that way—at least that's how I feel and have a lot different slant on life than I used to have. This war has undoubtedly changed me a lot in certain respects. If nothing else—I'm older—and certainly much wiser!"

Courtesy Cincinnati Museum Center/Cincinnati Historical Society Library

The following letter was found in the Cincinnati Historical Society's collection of World War II correspondence written by local soldiers. It does not contain a family name.

December 25, 1943

Dearest Mother:

In a sense all of us who belong in the family circle must find

a lump in our throats today—this isn't Christmas. At least not Christmas the way it's supposed to be. Shucks, we don't miss the presents, or the food, or the tree or anything else—what we miss is just the plain old business of being together at a time when our hearts are full of the happiness of being a family. What I miss is the look on Isabel's face—and yours, and Dad's and Dick's— just a good old look of plain happiness and gladness. Gladness for the things we have—the remembrances of our friends—and the tokens of deep feeling that we have had so much pleasure in giving to each other. But in spite of everything—I know that you stopped today and realized as I did just how much reason we do have for allowing our hearts to be filled with joy. If I wanted to I could easily convince myself that a dreary lonely Christmas is folding around me—but it is so much easier to admit that this has indeed been a rich Christmas—because I have thought, as I never have before not of the tinsel and wrapped packages but of all the gifts that you and Dad and now Isabel have given me throughout the years by just being who and what you are. I do miss all of you. All Love, Harry

Courtesy Cincinnati Museum Center/Cincinnati Historical Society Library

Soldiers opening package from home, Pietrmelara, Italy, December 16, 1943.

incinnati photographer Robert Flischel's uncle, Bob Flischel, was only eighteen when he went off to war. His unit was part of the 2nd Armored Division. A few days before Christmas he wrote a note to his parents.

Bob took part in the Battle of the Bulge and was injured on Christmas Day, 1944. He died a week later on New Year's

the Christmas tree, singing on Fountain Square, and visiting the crib in Lytle Park. Cincinnati was so glad to have them home.

The years following World War II were the victory years. Gone was anxiety for the boys at the front. Gone were ration cards, blackout curtains, and air raid warnings. It was time to celebrate. Back came metal toys, bikes, nylon stockings, gas,

Eve and his parents received the telegram above.

Bob Flischel joined the legions of young people who, since the founding of our country, gave all they had so that Americans now and in the future could live in freedom.

World War II ended in August 1945. By the following December, many of the service men and women were putting up

meat, and sugar. Back came the Christmas feast. Christmas tree lights that looked like bubbling candles were introduced. *It's a Wonderful Life* played at the Albee. Cincinnati Gas & Electric began displaying trains in their lobby. There was new hope and optimism in the air.

One of the young men who came home was James Coomer

(1928–2002). He had served in the navy and, as the son of a riverboat captain, felt right at home on a ship. After trying several other jobs, he ended up as a deckhand on a harbor tug. That was the beginning of a career on the Ohio river. He would spend almost thirty-five years on the river that means so much to Cincinnati and would learn the good side and the

Second Armored Division envelope.

Second Armored Division cover for letter.

bad side of its personality. There was Christmas on the water as well as on the land. The following chapter from Captain Coomer's memoir, *Life on the Ohio* (University Press of Kentucky, 1977), describes it well.

I have probably spent more Christmases afloat than on dry land. Except when I was a boy living on steamboats and at the yacht club, I spent them away from my family on a variety of craft in a variety of places: on a ship in the Whangpoo River at Shanghai, China, a ship in the Panama Canal, a ferry boat in Maine, a Norwegian freighter in New Orleans, a sailboat on Lake Erie, a houseboat on the Ohio River, a marina headboat (trying desperately to prevent it from taking an unauthorized trip down the river), and numerous tugboats and towboats.

On a towboat, where the crew is away from home for thirty days at a time, the men manage to pretend that Christmas is a matter of indifference to them. This is of course not true. Most would rather be with their families. The few days preceding Christmas are often as lonely as the holiday itself. In the evening as you pass the many lovely little river towns like Pomeroy, Gallipolis, Marietta, and Madison, you can see the Christmas trees and lights and busy shoppers and can sense the pleasant anticipation of all those folks on shore. The little red "Cold Beer" signs beckon, and you feel that you would give anything to be part of that happy throng. It is all a person can do to keep from tying off at the waterfront and jumping ship. And that has happened. It just becomes too much for some men.

Christmas mornings on the towboats we generally wished each other a Merry Christmas and griped a little about the cruel fate that separated us from loved ones, and that is about as far as our celebration went. There was seldom an exchange of presents, though over the years I have received several cartons of cigarettes and numerous bottles of aftershave. The most popular gift would have been bottles of cough medicine. When its alcoholic content was discovered, it accounted for more sudden "flu" epidemics on towboats, where booze is forbidden, than any Asian virus. The best gift we gave each other was a heightened camaraderie. We did for one day, this one special day, make an extra effort to be hearty and pleasant to our shipmates, and we donned clean work clothes. Slicker heads of hair and smoother jowls would not be seen on any other day of the year.

The holiday food was always special. On a boat that "feeds good," and most of them do, it is hard to imagine any improvement on daily fare. But on Christmas Day, the noon meal was something else: stick-to-the-ribs, gut-busting, down-home fare at its finest. It would include at least two meats, a fowl and a roast, plus three or four fresh vegetables, two kinds of salad, fresh fruit, pies, cake and ice cream, and a variety of drinks. It was all a person could do to stagger up to the pilothouse and stay awake during the next six hours of navigation.

It seemed to be a tradition also for towboats to "catch a willer," or tie off, wherever they might be, at about 11 a.m. on Christmas Day and not resume navigation until 11 p.m. This allowed the whole crew, both fore and aft watches, to eat together and share at least this one aspect of Christmas tradition.

The crew on a boat is really a family (at least on a happy ship), but because of alternating watches we do not get to know the men on the opposite watch very well.

I have seen about half a dozen Christmas trees on towboats. Sometimes I would see colored lights around the galley windows, and there were always a few boats with banners bearing the usual holiday salutations. I remember one with a Santa Claus, sleigh, and reindeer affixed to the stacks on the boiler deck. These displays were usually on boats that had elderly women cooks. Often widowed and with grown children, the cooks tended to shift their motherly affections to the boat crew, and many tried to duplicate as much as possible their Christ-

mas traditions and customs. Without them, Christmases afloat would indeed be dreary.

One Christmas on a boat I was running, we tied off a few miles above Meldahl Lock on the Ohio side. The river was very high and swift, and whole islands of driftwood were careening downstream. But we got a line out and settled in along the bank with no trouble. Our cook was a lovely lady named Virginia. Her Christmas meal was truly sumptuous, the galley had a small tree with lights and ornaments, and unbeknownst to us she had purchased an illicit pint of brandy on her last days off. Each crewmember found a small paper cup in front of his dinner plate, and Virginia carefully divided that pint of brandy twelve ways. It was a fine and thoughtful gesture, and we all appreciated it. I would believe that what happened later was proof positive that booze and boating don't mix, but my share of the alcohol amounted to only about three-fourths of an ounce.

At 1 p.m., we turned loose and started upriver. We had twelve empty tank barges and were bound for the refinery at Ashland, Kentucky. Even in this river stage, the trip ordinarily would take about thirty hours. Before we had been underway long, I had to make a crossover to get into slack water under a point. This required plowing through the drift, and as we did, a huge tree rolled out from under the tow and was swept under the boat. I immediately cut the power, but it was too late. The tree got into the propellers and rudders and sheared off a seven-foot-diameter, four-blade, stainless steel propeller. Shaft stub and wheel went to the bottom of the river. On half power, we barely made it to the refinery some seventy-eight hours later, and that was only with the help of another boat sent down to assist us.

Since the perils and demands of navigation do not stop for anything, Christmas is just another work day on the river. So most of us in the trade pretended that being out on the lonely water, and not with our families, was okay and just part of the job. But it was not a true feeling. On my boats the cook would often say a prayer at dinner, and the rough old river rats around the table would actually bow their heads and mumble "Amen." And if we happened to make a lock on Christmas Day, the lock's pay phone would have a long and anxious line of crew members waiting to touch home.

For no matter how positive and cheerful you try to make it, Christmas on towboats and cargo ships is a lonely time. And the one day of camaraderie cannot make up for the loneliness and longing, especially for children, whose holiday it is, after all. Even I, a fairly sensitive man, can only go through the usually bleak waterborne Christmases with, at best, playacting at good cheer, knowing full well that it is insincere. If you are lucky enough to get a turn at the phone it means more than all good food and short-term friendliness even found by those who choose to spend their lives on rivers or the seas.

Courtesy University Press of Kentucky

Christmas in the West End

Before Queensgate, before I-75, while there was still a Crosley Field, there was the West End. It was located northwest of the city and was at one time the literal end of the city. It had been the home of beer barons and factory owners. Later, it became home to the many African Americans who fled the South looking for work. James Brock grew up in the West End and remembers a West End Christmas in the 1950s:

We lived in a three-family house that had four bedrooms, two on the third floor, and two on the second floor. Sister Madison and her husband Mr. Wesley occupied the front bedroom on the third floor, and my aunt Margaret and her husband Bro. Clark occupied the third floor rear bedroom. We all shared the same dining room and kitchen. On the second floor, my parents were in the front bedroom facing the street, and all six of the children were in the rear bedroom facing the alley. My mother would start cooking the Christmas Day dinner on Christmas Eve and the smells that filled the entire house made you anxious for the next day to come. On Christmas morning we would all run downstairs to the first floor to see what Santa brought. We would not get multiple presents but usually one special thing such as a pair of shoes, a new pair of pants, or a toy that you might have longed for. One Christmas I remember getting a red wagon, and another Christmas, I got a bike. With six children, our parents sacrificed to make sure we had *at least one special gift every Christmas. And we always got a brown paper bag filled with nuts, an apple and orange, and other little goodies. In the afternoon we would go to church and give our speeches about the birth of Jesus followed by the singing of Christmas carols. Then we would rush back home to the Christmas feast: turkey and all the trimmings, sweet potato pie and the best coconut cake you've ever tasted. After dinner we would visit our friends to see what they got. Some of our friends didn't get anything so we would always share our toys with them. For a special treat, a bunch of us would sometimes go to the one house on the block that had a TV, that is, if it was working. Christmas was a special time of the year for us, and we dreamed about its coming months before it arrived. Sure, religious plays and speeches played a big part of what I remember, but to be totally honest, getting gifts and sharing them with friends played a bigger part.*

Cincinnati did not escape the tumult of the sixties and seventies: the years that a president was assassinated, boys went off to fight in the jungles of Vietnam and a president resigned. These were the years that young people questioned long-established values, that the struggle for the recognition of civil rights for all Americans would face some of its most crucial tests, and the years that women worked valiantly to gain legal and political equality.

Once again, through it all, Christmas with its message of peace and good will remained, calling us home to celebrate. The Christmas of 1973 was different, however. It was the Christmas with the lights out. The country was undergoing an energy crisis and Americans were being asked to conserve fuel and electricity. As a result, the lights and displays that had always been part of Christmas decorations were either cut back or eliminated. The shopping centers and malls did not light their decorations. The tree on Fountain Square was not filled with lights as it normally was. Homes that usually had outdoor decorations lost their glitter. It was Cincinnati's dark Christmas. The crisis did not last long, and by the following year the holiday lights returned.

During the last thirty years, Cincinnati has felt the repercussions of world events. The end of the Cold War brought momentary relief from constant vigilance and the hope that a lasting peace was at hand. When the World Trade Center was attacked on September 11, 2001, all those hopes were dashed. Now places whose names Cincinnati's forefathers would not recognize have made changes in the river city. Iraq, Iran, Afghanistan are part of everyday experience. Yet the city founded on the shores of the Ohio River at Christmastime has retained its Christmas spirit. Old traditions such as mechanical window displays, pantomimes, and bonfires have been replaced with new ones. Skating on Fountain Square, rappelling Santas, and carriage rides have become part of the holiday scene. Folks still sing about Christmas, go to see the trains, put a tree up on Fountain Square, visit the stable in Eden Park, and watch *The Nutcracker*, *A Christmas Carol*, and the Boar's Head Festival. The spirit of hospitality, peace, good will, and generosity binds the community together as Tiny Tim's words resonate across the seven hills,

"God bless us everyone."

The cast of *A Christmas Carol* at Cincinnati Playhouse in the Park.
Photo by Sandy Underwood.

Christmas

Cincinnatians have always loved music and incorporate it into all their celebrations, especially Christmas. They sing at Music Hall, in churches, at Fountain Square, in homes, at parties, and in their cars.

In 1935, the mayor joined carolers on Fountain Square while they sang the songs of hope and peace for everyone.

Mayor To Add To Many Accomplishments:
He Will Sing Carols On Fountain Square
His Honor Will Also Extend Greetings to Listeners at
Times-Star Party, December 24.

"It's a splendid idea to invite thousands of Cincinnatians to lift their voices in song on Christmas Eve," declared Wilson.

The mayor, who is a pretty good Christmas caroler, accepted the invitation of Theodore Hahn, of the committee in charge, to join in the singing. His honor will also extend welcome greetings to the assembled multitude at the opening of the sing, which is set for 3 p.m.

Mayor Wilson is a baritone and formerly sang in the May Festival chorus. All citizens, men, women, and children, are cordially invited to take part in the singing.

The Cincinnati Recreation Commission is among the many organizations to lend approval to the project. Director Tam Deering will co-operate in arranging for the yuletide decorations.

A Christmas tree, brilliant with colored lights, will add color and atmosphere to the scene.

Eugene Goossens, conductor of the Cincinnati Symphony Orchestra, is honorary chairman of the commit-

CULTURE
{Tradition}

tee in charge. The Program Committee, consisting of J. H. Thuman, R. R. Edwards and Hahn, announced Tuesday that one rehearsal will be held.

This rehearsal will take place Sunday, December 22, at 3 p.m. in the Taft Auditorium, Fred G. Flatt,

A group of prominent citizens comprising the Music Advisory Committee of the Works Progress Association, has general charge of the affair.

The committee has sent invitations to the following organizations to take part in the sing—but the invitations

manager of the Masonic Temple, having charge of the arrangements there.

Alfred Hartzel, chorus master of the May Festival, will conduct at the rehearsal and also at the sing on Fountain Square.

are general and are not limited to this list: Conservatory of Music, College of Music, Madisonville Music Club, Clifton Music Club, Wyoming Music Club, Y. W. C. A. Music Club, Western Hills Music Club, Bach Society, Hyde Park Music Club, Cincinnati Symphony Circle, Cincinnati Liter-

ary and Music Society, Monday Music Club, Three Arts Club, the Orpheus Club, U. of C. Men's Glee Club, Choir of Hebrew Union College, Grotto Choristers, Samuel W. Bell Home, Mothersingers, Hyde Park Choral Circle, Cincinnati Women's Club, Business Women's Glee Club, Fontbonne, Cincinnati Teachers' Chorus, Girls' Glee Club of U. C., Cincinnati May Festival Association, Herwegh Maennerchor, German Hungarian Choir, Jewish Center, Cincinnati Symphony Orchestra, Xavier Glee Club, WCKY Jubilee Singers, Plantation Farm, Charioteers, Carmel Female Chorus, Queen City Glee Club, Hosanna Singers, Lockland Glee Club, Melody Six, Negro Newsboy Choral Club, Y. M. C. A. Glee Club, Laymen's League Chorus, Weatherford Octet, Stowe School Mothers' Chorus, Harriet Beecher Stowe School Mothers, Dorcas Chorus, Hattie Jackson Guild, Zion Baptist Church, Cumminsville Choral and Dramatic Society, Mt. Zion Gospel Singers, West End Progressive Club, Young People's Choral Club, Sinton Singers, and Cincinnati Civic Opera.

Courtesy Cincinnati Museum Center/Cincinnati Historical Society Library, *Cincinnati Times-Star,* December 17, 1935.

May Festival Chorus Christmas Carols

Cincinnati Boychoir, 1984

Music Hall dressed for Christmas

Courtesy May Festival

This Christmas carol was written by Father John de Deo O.F.M. and for many years was a part of the Summit Country Day School's Christmas concert.

Sweet Babe Divine

Sweet babe Divine now Sleep,
While hovering angels keep
All hallowed vigil round Thy throne,
Adoring Thee alone.
From Thee that shining throng,
In glad triumphal song,
To men one happy message brings:
Behold the King of kings.
By all the world be He adored
Your Savior and your Lord.
This day, O Babe divine,
Make all love pure like Thine.
Let reign o'er all the world tonight
Sweet peace and love and light.

Courtesy Summit Country Day School

Window Displays

$\mathcal{I}$t used to be that it was not Christmas until the window displays appeared in the downtown stores. In 1928, John Shillito presented a window display that showed how Cincinnati looked ninety-nine years earlier, in 1829. The windows were so popular that Shillito's treated its customers and Cincinnati to more and more elaborate displays. The other department stores, Pogue's, Mabley & Carew, Rollman's, and McAlpin's joined the competition; all drew people to their stores with their window displays. Many Cincinnati families had a Christmas tradition of going to see the windows and then out to dinner at Wiggins or the Cricket.

In 1959, the theme for Shillito's window was Dickens's *A Christmas Carol*. Thirty-eight characters with four thousand moving parts were custom-made in Germany and shipped in sixteen crates. Six display personnel spent five days assembling the imports while five others wired the characters for animation. The window was a tremendous draw and people came from all over to see it.

One of Shillito's most memorable displays was Santa's workshop, usually set up in the window at Seventh and Elm. Mechanical elves were shown in the mailroom collecting letters to Santa, making toys, packing toys, painting toys, talking to Santa, and sometimes being mischievous. At times there were even live deer in the window. In the course of Shillito's being sold to Lazarus and then to Macy's, the elves were sold

to a Boy Scout troop and then to Bill Spinnenweber who has stored and protected them. They sit today, like the characters in *Toy Story*, waiting to give a Christmas performance. Noted Cincinnati photographer Robert Flischel captured their magic for us all.

The Crib of the Nativity

Of all the Cincinnati Christmas traditions, the stable in Eden Park is the most treasured. It all started with A. L. Heger, a Cincinnati landscape architect, who built a similar crèche on his property. The chairman of the board of Western and Southern Life Insurance, Charles Williams, admired it and asked Mr. Heger to build one in Lytle Park. Andy Biedenharn was working for Mr. Heger and was given the job of building the first crib scene; his family has been doing it ever since. And Western and Southern Financial Group has been sponsoring it ever since.

During World War II, the crèche was moved to Union Terminal so that servicemen could see it. After the war, it went back to Lytle Park and then to Eden Park.

Because it takes about a month to build the stable, the Biedenharn family begins work on the crèche before Thanksgiving. The stable is made of hand-hewn logs and features a thatched roof made with real straw. The wax figures wear handmade garments and add realism to the scene. When the stable is completed, the animals are brought in. Jim Tutman provides a Jersey cow known for its gentleness. For twenty years the donkey, Pedro, was given the star animal role. He was a family pet of the Biedenharn's and is buried on their farm. The Walton Horse Farm now provides a donkey. Sara is ready for her role, groomed and looking like a star. Jody Biedenharn, part of the third generation of the family, says that Pedro always knew when it was time to go to the stable. "The animals like to come," she says. "They are curious about the people." Sheep have been part of the scene for the past thirty years. The sound of their bells and their bleating remind visitors of the simplicity of the first Christmas.

The Biedenharns make many sacrifices to bring this beloved tradition to Cincinnati. Some member of the family must be at the stable around the clock. Because of this, they have their family Christmas at 5:30 a.m. Jody says taking care of the stable requires some sacrifice, but it does have rewards. Her biggest treat is to hear a child's delight when she sees the Baby Jesus for the first time. "They get excited," she says, but then they always ask, "What stinks?"

There is an unsolved mystery at the stable. Every Christmas Eve a twenty-dollar bill is found tucked in Jesus' swaddling clothes. The Biedenharns have never been able to identify who left it. It is a Christmas mystery.

Over the past seventy-two years, more than two million people have visited the crib. The scene gives reality to the Christmas story and for many, a visit to the crib and then to the Krohn is an important part of their family's Christmas tradition.

Donations at the display are matched by the Western and Southern Foundation. These contributions help needy children and the homeless through the Salvation Army.

70   Cincinnati Christmas

In churches and homes throughout the Cincinnati area it is a tradition to remember the first Christmas by displaying the Christmas crèche. Pictured above is the crèche at St. Francis de Sales Church in East Walnut Hills. Built in 1878 this beautiful Church is a landmark at the corner of Woodburn and Madison roads.

Duke Energy trains. Photo by Tom Wolfe, courtesy Duke Energy.

Trains

The model trains that are displayed in the lobby of the Duke Energy building have become one of the most popular holiday events in downtown Cincinnati, delighting more than two hundred thousand visitors each year.

Started in 1946 by Cincinnati Gas & Electric, the display grew larger each year. In the 1980s, CG&E made a commitment to the long-term renovation and expansion of the display. Today, the display is thirty-six feet wide by forty-seven feet long.

A small group of Duke Energy employees handcraft replacement parts and add to the collection of miniature structures throughout the year. Assembly of the trains takes about thirty days. They are precisely scaled-sized and historically accurate. Fifty engines feature both steam and diesel engines.

A visit to see the train display is very much a Cincinnati Christmas tradition.

The Cincinnati Museum Center also presents a display of model trains at the original and beautiful Union Terminal. Holiday Junction brings trains, trains, and more trains for children and adults to enjoy.

Cincinnati Times-Star, December 22, 1948.

Holiday Junction. Courtesy Cincinnati Museum Center

The Boar's Head Festival

King Wenceslas and his pages sing the traditional Christmas carol.

Legend has it that in 1340, a scholar in Oxford, England, was walking through a forest reading Aristotle on his way to Christmas Mass when a large and angry boar attacked him. Defending himself, he threw his metal-bound book down the beast's throat. That did the trick; the boar choked to death, and that night its head, dressed and garnished, was carried into the Queen's College dining room surrounded by carolers. The Boar's Head Festival, expanded to include lords, ladies, knights, cooks, hunters, shepherds, and wise men, has been celebrated at Oxford ever since.

A French Huguenot family named Bouton imported the seeds of the tradition to Troy, New York, in colonial times when they immigrated there to escape religious persecution. They had experienced the Boar's Head Festival during a stay in England. One of their descendants became rector of the Episcopal Hoosac School near Troy and in 1888 he established the festival there as an annual event in the school dining hall.

In 1939, when the Reverend Nelson Burroughs came to Cincinnati from Troy to be the rector of Christ Church Cathedral, he brought with him the tradition of the Boar's Head Festival, presenting it in a church setting for the first time.

Every aspect of the production must be as authentic to the fourteenth-century as possible. The performance must take place between Christmas and New Year's Day and the food must be homemade. Since it is hard to find a boar's head in Cincinnati, a hog's head is substituted, carried in on a trencher with an apple in its mouth.

Today, the Christ Church cast numbers over 170, with another seventy people in the choir and orchestra and another seventy working behind the scenes. About a hundred churches throughout the United States now have their own Boar's Head Festival.

This living story of Christ's victory over evil is a glorious gift from Christ Church Cathedral to the people of Cincinnati every Christmas season.

The Beefeaters, the traditional guards of the Tower of London, await their turn on stage.

Adoration of the shepherds.

The chief minstrel sings the fourteenth-century Boar's Head carol.

The Nutcracker

Since 1975, Tchaikovsky's beloved *Nutcracker* has been presented by the Cincinnati Ballet, delighting children and adults. Dancing snowflakes, waltzing flowers, mischievous mice, and brave toy soldiers who have all practiced for months, bring the story of Marie and her toy soldier to life. Featuring outstanding choreography, magical sets and our own Cincinnati Symphony Orchestra, this is a holiday tradition cherished by all of Cincinnati. Frisch's, another Cincinnati favorite, sponsors this special event.

The Festival of Lights

As winter arrives, the Cincinnati Zoo adorns itself in holiday lights that make it sparkle up and down, over and under. Even the lake is twinkling. It is a wondrous event.

Puppets, reindeer, Santa, the North Pole Village, a gingerbread man, hot cocoa all add to the spirit of Christmas. Many of the zoo animals are part of the show, as well.

Sponsored by PNC Bank, the Festival of Lights is another of Cincinnati's great traditions.

THE FESTIVAL OF

Lights

A Christmas Carol

Since 1981, Playhouse in the Park has been producing Charles Dickens's *A Christmas Carol*. This timeless story of a curmudgeon who finally finds the true spirit of Christmas has taken its place as one of Cincinnati's great holiday traditions. Staging, costumes, music, and sets magically bring the story to life and send everyone home with a smile on their face and a better understanding of the words "God bless us everyone."

Below: Amy Warner is Mrs. Fezziwig and Keith Jochim is Mr. Fezziwig in the Cincinnati Playhouse in the Park's production of *A Christmas Carol*. Photo by Sandy Underwood.

Right: Todd Lawson is the Ghost of Christmas Future and Bruce Cromer is Ebenezer Scrooge in the Cincinnati Playhouse in the Park's production of *A Christmas Carol*. Photo by Sandy Underwood.

Poinsettias

Poinsettias, poinsettias, poinsettias! The plant is everywhere in Cincinnati at Christmas; in churches, homes, and stores. Native to Mexico, the plant was introduced by Joseph Poinsett to the United States in 1825. Today it makes up 85 percent of plant sales during the holiday season.

Above: Margaret Rahn and Susan Rahn Patten, sisters, in front of their beautiful poinsettias at the A. J. Rahn greenhouse.

Right: A tree of poinsettias at the Krohn Conservatory.

Angels in the City

Cincinnati has angels all over the city. Some say that they, too, have a tradition. At two o'clock in the morning on Christmas Day, they quickly and quietly begin to move and then they all fly to the top of the Suspension Bridge where they joyfully sing together for about an hour. When you cross the bridge, you can hear them singing.

Praying Angel (1848) by Odoardo Fantacchiotti. Cincinnati Art Museum. Gift by the Archbishop of Cincinnati, from the Cathedral of St. Peter in Chains and St. Teresa of Avila Catholic Church, Price Hill. Accession #s 1998.59 and 1998.60

Adoring Angel (1849) by Odoardo Fantacchiotti.

Far left: Carrara marble angel with font, Mother of God Church, Covington, Kentucky, 1921.

Left top: Detail of angel wing St. Ursula Academy Chapel, Walnut Hills.

Left bottom: Guardian Angel, Guardian Angels School gym, Mount Washington.

Above: Angels, Cathedral Basilica of the Assumption, Covington, Kentucky. Murals painted by Frank Duveneck and dedicated to his mother, 1910.

Right: The Emery Angel was commissioned in 1898 by Thomas and Mary Emery. It originally held a clamshell and served as a baptismal font at Christ Church Cathedral. In 1955 it was moved to Spring Grove Cemetery. The photographer has supplied the angel's Christmas presents.

Angels, Cathedral Basilica of the Assumption, Covington, Kentucky.

Christmas

Columbia Christmas Feast

Columbia-Tusculum, formerly called Columbia, located on the river approximately five miles east of downtown Cincinnati, was founded about one month before the Cincinnati founders appeared. Those folks had time to get a Christmas dinner together, and they invited Native Americans living in the area to join them. A long table was set up outdoors near the river and stew was cooked in two large kettles hung over a good fire. Since the area was overflowing with wild turkeys, they were probably on the menu as well. Berries, nuts, corn, apples, cranberries, and pies would have been part of the feast, too.

In 1796, Amelia Simmons published a book called:

The First American Cookbook
By Amelia Simmons
an American Orphan

Her recipe for roasting a turkey:

To Stuff and Roast a Turkey or Fowl—One pound soft wheat bread, three ounces beef suet, three eggs, a little sweet thyme, sweet marjoram, pepper and salt, and some add a gill of wine: fill the bird therewith and sew up, hang down to a steady solid fire, basting frequently with salt and water, and roast until a steam emits from the breast; put one third of a pound of butter into the gravy, dust flour over the bird and baste with the gravy; serve up with boiled onions and cranberry sauce, mangoes, pickles or celery.

F E A S T
{Food}

Others omit the sweet herbs and add parsley done with potatoes. Boil and mash three pints potatoes, wet them with butter, add sweet herbs, pepper, salt, fill and roast as above.

Wild Turkey, male, painted by John James Audubon, (American, 1785-1851) *Birds of America*, 1826.
From the collection of the Cincinnati and Hamilton County Public Library

A nineteenth century painting depicting the
Fifth Street Market House. Artist unknown.
Courtesy Cincinnati Museum Center/Cincinnati
Historical Society Library

Fifth Street Market House

By the mid-nineteenth century, Cincinnati had many market houses that were patronized by the growing population. The following description of the Fifth Street Market on Christmas Day appears in *Sketches and Statistics of Cincinnati* in 1851 published that year by local journalist Charles Cist. The market was open on Christmas because Christmas was not yet a legal holiday and would not be until 1870.

Markets and Market-Houses

Christmas day is the great gala day of the butchers of Cincinnati. The parade of stall-fed meat on that day, for several years past, has been such as to excite the admiration and astonishment of every stranger in Cincinnati—a class of persons always here in great numbers. The exhibition, this last year, has, however, greatly surpassed every previous display in this line.

A few days prior to the return of this day of festivity, the noble animals which are to grace the stalls on Christmas eve, are paraded through the streets, decorated in fine style, and escorted through the principal streets with bands of music and attendant crowds, especially of the infantry. They are then taken to slaughter-houses, to be seen no more by the public, until cut up and distributed along the stalls of one of our principal markets.

Christmas falling last year on Tuesday, the exhibition was made at what is termed our middle or Fifth Street market-house. This is three hundred and eighty feet long, and of breadth and height proportionate—wider and higher, in fact, in proportion to length, than the eastern market-houses. It comprehends sixty stalls, which, on this occasion, were filled with steaks and ribs alone, so crowded, as to do little more than display half the breadth of the meat, by the pieces overlapping each other, and affording only the platforms beneath the stall and the table, behind which the butcher stands, for the display of the rounds and other parts of the carcass. One hundred and fifty stalls would not have been too many to have been fully occupied by the meat exhibited on that day, in the manner beef is usually hung up here and in the eastern markets.

Sixty-six bullocks, of which probably three-fourths were raised and fed in Kentucky, and the residue in our own State; one hundred and twenty-five sheep, hung up whole at the edges of the stalls; three hundred and fifty pigs, displayed in rows on platforms; ten of the finest and fattest bears Missouri could produce; and a buffalo calf, weighing five hundred pounds, caught at Santa Fe, constituted the materials for this Christmas pageant. The whole of the beef was stall-fed, some of it since the cattle had been calves, their average age being four years, and average weight sixteen hundred pounds, ranging from 1,388, the lightest, to 1,896, the heaviest. This last was four years old, and had taken the premium every year at exhibitions in Kentucky, since it was a calf. The sheep were Bakewell and

Southdown, and ranged from ninety to one hundred and ninety pounds to the carcass, dressed and divested of the head, &c. The roasters or pigs would have been considered extraordinary anywhere but at Porkopolis, the grand emporium of hogs. Suffice to say, they did no discredit to the rest of the show. Bear meat is a luxury unknown at the East, and is comparatively rare here. It is the ne plus ultra of table enjoyment.

The extraordinary weight of the sheep will afford an idea of their condition for fat. As to the beef, the fat on the flanks measured seven and one-quarter inches, and that on the rump, six and one half inches through. A more distinct idea may be formed by the general reader, as to the thickness of the fat upon the beef, when he learns that two of the loins, on which were five and a half inches of fat, became tainted, because the meat could not cool through in time; and this, when the thermometer had been at no period higher than thirty-six degrees, and ranging, the principal part of the time, from ten to eighteen degrees above zero. This fact, extraordinary as it appears, can be amply substantiated by proof.

Specimens of these articles were sent by our citizens to friends abroad. The largest sheep was purchased by F. Ringgold, of the St. Charles, and forwarded whole to Philadelphia. Coleman of the Burnet House, forwarded to his brother of the Astor House, New York, nine ribs of beef, weighing one hundred and twenty pounds; and Richard Bates, a roasting piece of sixty-six pounds, by way of New Year's gift, to David T. Disney, our representative in Congress.

The Philadelphians and New Yorkers confessed that they never had seen anything in the line to compare with the specimens sent to those points.

The beef, &c., was hung up on the stalls early upon Christmas eve, and by twelve o'clock next day, the whole stock of beef—weighing 99,000 pounds—was sold out; two-thirds of it at that hour being either prepared for the Christmas dinner, or already consumed at the Christmas breakfast. It may surprise an eastern epicure to learn that such beef could be afforded to customers for eight cents per pound, the price at which it was retailed, as an average.

No expense was spared by our butchers to give effect to this great pageant. The arches of the market-house were illuminated by chandeliers and torches, and lights of various descriptions were spread along the stalls. Over the stalls were oil portraits—in gilt frames—of Washington, Jackson, Taylor, Clay, and other public characters, together with landscape scenes. Most of these were originals, or copies by our best artists. The decorations and other items of special expense these public-spirited men were at, reached in cost one thousand dollars. The open space of the market-house was crowded early and late by the coming and going throng of the thousands whose interest in such an exhibition overcame the discouragement of being in the open air at unseasonable hours, as late as midnight, and before daylight in the morning, and the thermometer at fifteen degrees.

We owe this exhibition to the public spirit of Vanaken and Daniel Wunder, John Butcher, J. & W. Gall, Francis and

Richard Beresford, among our principal victualers.

No description can convey to a reader the impression which such a spectacle creates. Individuals from various sections of the United States and from Europe, who were here—some of them Englishmen, and familiar with Leadenhall market—acknowledged they had never seen any show of beef at all comparable with this.

Charles Cist, *Sketches and Statistics of Cincinnati in 1851*, Cincinnati: Wm. H. Moore & Co., 1851, pp. 275-77.

Today, Findlay Market, just north of downtown, is the cherished spot in Cincinnati for good shopping in a diverse atmosphere. Founded in 1852, it retains the charm of yesterday and brings people from all over to shop in a lively, food-filled space in the heart of the city. It shines during the holidays as people prepare for their grand Christmas feast.

Celebrations

The *Cincinnati Enquirer* printed the following article on January 1, 1930. It is a first-hand account of a New Year's celebration and the food served in 1872.

Enjoy!

New Year's Reception in Cincinnati, 1872
by Alfred Gaither

"*Ah, New Year's Eve, that was the great time in our day,*" *sighed Grandfather as he watched us planning to celebrate this festival at one of the big hotels downtown where the latest jazz band would play those tantalizing tunes for dancing.*

Tureen made by the nineteenth-century Cincinnati silversmiths Duhme & Co.

Cincinnati Art Museum. Museum purchase: John S. Conner Endowment, Mark P. Herschede Endowment and Dwight J. Thomson Endowment.1999.207.

As twilight fell and we had made up our minds what each of us girls would wear and who should be asked to join our crowd, we asked Grandfather to tell us again about the times when forty-eight members of the family sat down to Christmas dinner and it took not only a shoat, hundreds of oysters, quail, a huge terrapin, but five or six huge turkeys to grace the feast of those days.

But the tale of the New Year's reception that was traditional in our ancestral home held fascinations all its own and we were ever ready to hear about it. Grandfather's home had been one of those great old places that now have given way to modern office buildings, the rooms on the first floor could all be thrown into one about twenty by ninety feet and here was held the New Year's reception to which every gentleman of rank and position in Cincinnati came and paid his respects to Grandmother and Grandfather.

For this occasion preparations began early in the autumn when we returned after a summer in the mountains or at the sea shore. Mother would personally supervise the putting up of fruit, pickles, jams and preserves, even the making of sausage, while Father personally selected the hams and sides of bacons and watched over the preparations necessary before they were taken to be smoked at "Old Man Gowder's" smokehouse. It also was cured his own special way, hence the baked hams at the New Year's receptions were in great favor as they had a flavor all their own. At this time the fruit cakes were being baked, placed in tin cans whose tops could be lifted off when the brandy was poured over the cakes each week to keep them in good condition and fine flavor.

Just before the holidays great barrels of oysters came from Baltimore and Norfolk; hindquarters of venison came from Virginia; terrapin—yes, they were alive—from Maryland; prairie chicken from Illinois; wild turkey from Virginia; scallops from Massachusetts; and quail from nearer home.

We had a wonderful cellar which Mother had divided into special compartments for these different food stuffs. There was a part with brine containing troughs of water into which the terrapin were turned loose and fed on celery tops until such a time as they were needed by the cook. There was a bin into which the oysters were placed, bowl of shell down, and fed three times a day with cornmeal brine.

The game was hung from the ceiling in a cooling room, but it did not hang long for we had many guests from the 23d of December through January 2d. When we were all together for Christmas we were 28 to sit down to dinner, and the evening before, this was in 1872. Uncle Tom had to take us down to the Old National Theater, on Sycamore Street, between Fourth and Third, to see Humpty Dumpty, so we were out of the way for the tree-trimming business. What a time we had getting there— and it was but a few blocks—and getting settled; I really believe we did not get really settled until the play was almost over, and then we did not remember much about it, because we were more interested in wondering what Santa Claus was doing at home with so much mystery that we had to be bundled out of the house.

But New Year's was the great day and the traditions of our reception were established and known throughout the city, and were kept up in our beautiful home at 409 Broadway until my mother's death.

Mother always had some of her young lady friends to assist her in receiving the guests in the front drawing room, where they stood against a background of beautiful holiday greens and brilliant flowers. The picture these lovely young ladies made in their charming gowns and happy smiles made a deep impression on our youthful memory.

In the dining room the long table was decorated with a wonderful set of gorgeous Bohemian glass of a cherry red color with gold edges. The large epergne in the center was filled with flowers, the smaller epergnes to either side held fruit, and the four compotes at the corners held candy. Stacks of plates and saucers flanked these.

At one end of the table was a massive silver chafing dish containing a steaming terrapin a la Maryland. My father was famous for the preparation of this dish. The huge chafing dish at the other end was filled with broiled quail, each one plump and served appetizingly on a square of toast. On one side was a chafing dish in which were heaped and kept sizzling hot oysters that had been fried in olive oil, a simply delicious tidbit, not only to our taste but to that of our guests, too. On the other side of the table stood a large-boned turkey wonderful in its decorated coat of aspic. Then there were bowls of chicken, sweetbread and lobster salads, trays of tiny biscuits as large as a half dollar, light as a feather and piping hot from the oven every five minutes or so. Alongside these was the baked ham, while a smoking hot dish of scalloped oysters stood at the opposite corner. In between were dishes of pickles, jams, salted almonds, pistachio nuts and thinly sliced fruit cakes.

Besides Charles, our butler, the servants were reinforced by three or four perfect waiters, men trained in Southern homes to housework, the like of whom you cannot find today. One man especially I remember distinctly, for he was at other times the preacher at the Allan Temple at Sixth and Broadway and his name was *Peter Fossett. Another was a baker down on Fourth Street, and the others also worked at various trades during the year. However, for special parties, receptions and such events, these men were in great demand and had to be engaged almost six months ahead.

These men served the hot dishes to the guests as they came to the table; there was no confusion, everything went like clockwork and we children knew we had to mind our P's and Q's if we wanted to stay downstairs during the hours of festivity.

On a table near a window rested an old English glass bowl of the same red color as the table set, this one, however, was an heirloom and I had heard my father tell that he remembered his grandfather using it on New Year's Day. It stood on three legs, was huge and pot-bellied, tapering to a small mouth, and was surrounded by 24 mugs of the same general outline and sitting on three legs each. The great bowl was filled with eggnog and beside it was a smaller beautiful Venetian green and gold glass

bowl filled with champagne punch. This table was presided over by my father, who greeted his friends as they approached the table. As this panorama of long ago passes my mind's eye there comes into view the familiar faces of many of our friends, men famous in their time—railroad officials, lawyers, doctors, bankers, statesmen, newspaper men—all leading men in the city. There were Dr. Dandridge, Julius Dexter, William H. Harrison, Elliott Pendleton, Senator George Pendleton, Mathew Addy, William Ludlow, William Schoenberger, Thomas Emery, Murat Halstead, "Deacon" Richard Smith, Theodore Cook, Colonel Joseph McDowell, John Shillito, Henry Probasco, Henry Hanna, Charles P. Taft, C. T. Woodrow and many other whose names spell the history and progress of Cincinnati.

Of one prominent clubman the story was told that he refused dinner invitations for at least three days before New Year's because, he said, he "wished to do justice to what he knew awaited him at Tom Gaither's." And another story goes that this same wag answered his beautiful dinner partner when she asked him: "Major, will you please tell me how you can tell the difference between a canvas-back duck and a red head when served?" "Only one way, madame, and that is by the bill."

Another feature of the New Year's Day celebration was the friendly rivalry between the Regulars and Independents for the Mercantile Library election. Usually the young men brought in huge posters advertising their candidates and besought their friends to vote for them. The annual fight between the Regulars and Independents was always a great social event, the election *taking place early in January. The lady members voted at the library, while the gentlemen voted at the Chamber of Commerce, but all of the society was keenly interested in the event.*

As the reception lasted from 5 to 7 o'clock the story is told of some of our friends who so much appreciated our cuisine that they came early and remained late for another round of the good things, and if we could enjoy such a wonderful array of delicacies in our own home today I am sure the delightful custom of holding a New Year's reception for our friends would still hold. It was the acme of hospitality and an event looked forward to from January 2 to the next New Year's Day.

With permission of the *Cincinnati Enquirer*
Courtesy Cincinnati Museum Center/Cincinnati Historical Society Library
Gift of Mrs. NDC Hodges, November 25,1935

*Peter Fossett had been Thomas Jefferson's slave. When Mr. Jefferson died Peter was sold on the auction block. Eventually he made his way to his family and freedom in Cincinnati. He started a catering business, became a community leader, served on the board of the city's segregated school system, assisted the Underground Railroad and was a Captain in the Black Brigade. He was ordained a Baptist minister and served his Church for many years. —JB

The Bakers

And then there are the bakers. Cincinnati has a long history of the very best. There are few cities in the country where you can find the quality that these wonderful artisans bring us. Christmas is the time for them to shine, and shine they do.

The BonBonerie. Mary Pat Pace and Sharon Butler established this bakery in O'Bryonville in 1983 and it has thrived ever since. Christmas goodies are plentiful and tasty.

Top left: Yule log from the BonBonerie, O'Bryonville.

Top right: Happy Holidays Cake from the BonBonerie.

Left: Gingerbread men from the BonBonerie.

Graeter's, a Cincinnati institution since 1870, is best known for its ice cream, and peppermint is perfect for Christmas. There are lots of other Graeter's Christmas goodies that Cincinnatians scoop up for great Christmas sweets.

IRRESISTIBLE

SINCE
Graeter's
1870

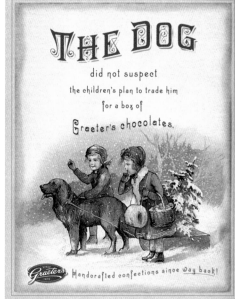

THE DOG

did not suspect
the children's plan to trade him
for a box of
Graeter's chocolates.

SINCE
Graeter's
1870
Handcrafted confections since way back!

Graeter's ads

When Norma
DISCOVERS
the elves haven't brought
any Graeter's chocolates,
teeny-tiny heads will roll.

SINCE
Graeter's
1870
Handcrafted confections since way back!

Graeter's
peppermint
ice cream

Graeter's fruitcake

Servatii's has specialized in authentic German baked goods since it first opened in Hyde Park in 1963 and at Christmas they are extra special: Yule logs, tea cookies, gingerbread houses, stollen and German cookies. Danke schoen, Servatii's.

Servatii's Little Greg and gingerbread

Servatii's gingerbread house

Servatii's chocolate mousse cake

Melissa Mileto brought Take the Cake to Northside six years ago. The bakery specializes in extraordinary cakes that are very special. And now Take the Cake also serves a tasty lunch.

Busken, a Cincinnati name since the 1930s, produces Christmas treats that Cincinnati longs for: tea cookies, schnecken, sugar cookies, fruitcakes, pies and gingerbread men. They advertise their sugar delights on billboards that give a clever and appealing message: "Enjoy life because life is funny. And while you are at it treat yourself to a little reward."

Fountain Square

Christmas Eve in Clifton
by Frederick Thomas

It was late Christmas Eve
Snow covered the park,
The moon lit the fountain
In spite of the dark.

Skyline was near closing
A few clients stayed,
The cooks hoped to leave
When the last one had paid.

All heard a loud screech
As a car braked real hard,
To avoid a huge sleigh
Which came down in the yard.

Tom was stirring the chili
And warming the buns,
When through the front door
Came a dude, quite rotund.

He moved with real grace
And was dressed all in red,
A beard hid his costume
From his belt to his head.

The guests, they just gaped
As well they all should,
Such things just don't happen
Around Burnet Wood!

He laughed a great laugh
As he went down his list,
Perched his glasses just right
To see what he'd missed.

"For Donner a three-way
And for Cupid a four,
For Comet no onions
But for Dancer lots more!

"A Burrito for Dasher
Extra cheese, please, for Vixen,
For Prancer, two coneys
And a two-way for Blitzen."

"Please make it 'to go'
We're on a great quest,
With much to deliver
Before we can rest."

Tom never had seen
The cooks move so fast,

In the blink of an eye
Santa had his repast.

He paid with a smile
And quickly he stood,
By his sleigh full of toys
For kids who were good.

There was a great wind
And a clatter of hooves,
And the bells on the sleigh
Down Ludlow they moved!

We ran out to see
As they sailed through the night,
Their tummies were filled
What a magical sight!

And Tom, he just smiled
With a tear and a sigh,
After decades at Skyline
Now he'd seen reindeer fly!

We heard them shout out
As they flew out of sight,
"Merry Christmas, dear Clifton
And to all a good night!"

When ex-Cincinnatians come home for Christmas one of the first places they head to is a chili parlor.

Favorite Christmas Recipes of Cincinnati Chefs

Cincinnati has always loved to eat, and the city has been blessed with many fine chefs who work hard to please and satisfy.

Marilyn's Pecan Pie
by Marilyn Harris

"A restaurant in town served this pie with great success after I had done some consulting work for them, and I actually had the temerity to serve it to Albert Roux (French restauranteur) when he came to my house for dinner," Marilyn recalls. *"He said he liked it. I do, too, and so I have attached my name to it. Having grown up in the South, I have tasted more than my share of pecan pies and have experimented with many recipes over the years—this is my favorite. My first attempt at making a pecan pie was instructive, if a bit embarrassing. In graduate school I was trying to impress my husband-to-be, who loved pecan pies. I pierced the pastry as I was accustomed to do for 'icebox' pies, put the pecan filling in, and baked it. The final product was very strange: the liquid filling ran through the crust. There was filling on the bottom, crust in the middle, and pecans on top. He married me anyway, but the moral is: Never pierce the pastry for a liquid-filling pie. This pie has both light and dark corn syrup for just the right balance of flavor and four extra-large eggs to yield a lighter custard rather than one with a heavy, sticky texture. The pastry is a French derivation of a pâte brisée, the same type of pastry used in French tarts. Since it takes this dense mixture so long to cool, make this pie several hours ahead."*

9-inch unbaked pastry shell (recipe follows)

4 tablespoons unsalted butter, softened

1 cup sugar

1 tablespoon flour

1 cup light corn syrup

1 cup dark corn syrup

Pinch salt

4 extra-large eggs

1¼ cups pecan halves

1 teaspoon vanilla extract

Make pastry shell.

Cream butter with electric mixer. Add sugar and flour and cream until fluffy. Add both syrups and the pinch of salt. Beat until smooth. Add eggs, one at a time, beating well after each addition. Fold in the pecans and vanilla. Pour into the pastry shell. Bake in the bottom third of a preheated 350° oven 1 hour and 10 minutes or until puffed and golden brown.

Serves 8 to 10.

Pastry

1½ cups unbleached or pastry flour
½ teaspoon salt
1 large egg yolk
1 stick (4 ounces) very cold unsalted butter
5 tablespoons ice water

Place the flour, salt and egg yolk in food processor with steel blade. Cut the butter into 8 or 9 pieces and add. Blend until mixture resembles coarse meal. Add ice water and blend until a dough forms. Knead on a lightly floured surface with the heel of your hand until a smooth ball of dough forms. Press into a disc. Place in a plastic bag and chill at least 2 hours. Let sit at room temperature about 20 minutes, or until pliable enough to roll easily. Using a pastry rolling pin, roll out on a lightly floured surface to about 1/8 inch thick. Place the rolling pin on one edge of the pastry and quickly roll the pastry onto the pin. Unroll over top of the pie pan. Gently press into the pan. Trim and crimp the top edges.

If a food processor is not available, place the dry ingredients in a shallow mixing bowl. Add cold butter and cut in with two table knives with serrated edges, cutting in an X fashion. Beat egg yolk into the ice water. Make a well in center of the dry mixture and pour in the liquid. Blend quickly with fingertips and proceed as directed above.

Chilling the dough accomplishes several things: It allows it to "rest" so that the gluten in the flour relaxes, which makes it easier to roll and less likely to shrink when placed in a hot oven. Chilling also causes the little flakes of butter to set and result in a flakier baked pastry. And, last but not least, the chilled pastry is easier to handle while rolling and placing in the pan.

Roasted Venison Loin
by Todd Kelly

"I do a version of this dish every year at Orchids, the restaurant in the Netherland Plaza Hotel downtown," says Todd. "One year I had just finished Thanksgiving dinner with my family and made the statement that I like canned cranberry sauce. Although I also like chutneys and homemade cranberry sauces, I enjoy the texture and the sweetness of the canned. So then I started to work on a recipe that would look like the canned kind but have a unique flavor. I came up with vanilla and cardamom. I add some agar powder to keep the melting temperature higher so we can serve it on a warm plate without having it melt. The chestnuts and salsify just remind me of Christmas, and the mulled wine ties it all together."

For the venison:

4 venison loins, 6 ounces each

1 quart water

¼ cup sugar

¼ cup salt

½ cup gin

4 juniper berries

Remove silver skin from the venison. Combine the water, sugar and salt in a large saucepan. Cook until the sugar and salt are dissolved. Cool, then add the gin and juniper berries and the venison. Marinate the venison for 3 hours.

For the cranberry sauce:

1 bag fresh cranberries

1 quart water

2 cups sugar

5 cardamom pods, cracked

1 vanilla bean, split

5 teaspoons agar powder

6 gelatin sheets, bloomed

Simmer cranberries, water, sugar, cardamom and vanilla until cranberries are tender. Puree in a blender and strain. Bring 1 quart of the mixture to room temperature and add agar. Simmer 3 minutes, stirring constantly. Add gelatin and simmer 1 more minute. Strain and pour into a vessel or vessels for cooling. I use 2-inch-diameter PVC pipes cut 3 inches high.

For the chestnuts:

1 pound fresh chestnuts, roasted and peeled

2 cups heavy cream

Lightly simmer the chestnuts in cream until they are soft. Add water if the cream starts to thicken. Strain the chestnuts and reserve the liquid. Place the soft chestnuts in blender and puree until smooth, adding liquid as needed to create a smooth paste. Season with salt and white pepper.

For the salsify:

8 ounces fresh salsify

1 lemon

1 cup flour

2 eggs, beaten

1 cup almonds, finely chopped

Vegetable oil for frying

Peel the salsify and cut into large julienne. Squeeze the lemon into a bowl of water and place the salsify in the water to prevent it from oxidizing. Cook the salsify in gently simmering water until tender. Cool. Dip each salsify piece in the flour and remove excess, then dip in the egg and roll in almonds. Heat the oil in a fryer set at 350°. Fry the salsify until golden brown. Remove from the fryer and season with salt.

For the mulled wine jus:

2 cups red wine

1 cup ruby port wine

4 juniper berries

½ cinnamon stick

3 whole cloves

2 whole star anise

1 quart chicken stock

In a saucepan combine all of the ingredients minus the chicken stock and simmer until liquid is reduced to 1 cup. Add the stock and cook 20 minutes, or until desired consistency and flavor are reached. Strain the mixture and keep warm.

To serve:

Heat some oil in a sauté pan over medium heat. Season the venison with salt and pepper and sear until golden brown on all sides. Place the venison in a 350° oven until its internal temperature reaches 100°. Allow to rest 5 minutes. Place the cylinder(s) of cranberry sauce in the center of a warm serving plate. Shape the chestnut puree into quenelles and place them next to the cranberry sauce. Place the salsify next to the chestnut quenelles. Slice the venison into thin slices and shingle around the cranberry sauce. Drizzle the plate with the mulled wine jus.

Serves 4.

Queen City Crab Cakes
by Beth O'Leary

Beth O'Leary Catering in Newtown helps families, friends, and businesses celebrate the season with a variety of good and tasty foods. "Over the holidays, crab cakes are very popular, especially for Christmas," she says. "I guess people feel that they can splurge and spoil themselves a little bit." Go ahead, spoil yourself.

4 tablespoons unsalted butter, melted and cooled

4 large eggs, lightly beaten

6 tablespoons sour cream

¼ cup minced fresh parsley

2 tablespoons fresh lemon juice

1 teaspoon Worcestershire sauce

1 teaspoon paprika

½ teaspoon salt, or to taste

¼ teaspoon cayenne, or to taste

2 pounds lump crabmeat, picked over

2 cups fine fresh breadcrumbs

⅓ cup cornmeal

½ cup vegetable oil

Tarragon Tartar Sauce (recipe follows)

Lemon wedges

Whisk together the butter, eggs, sour cream, parsley, lemon juice, Worcestershire, paprika, salt and cayenne. Gently stir in crabmeat and breadcrumbs. Form ½-cup measures of the mixture into 12 cakes, each ¾ inch thick. Place the cakes in a baking dish that has been sprinkled with half the cornmeal. Sprinkle the cakes with the remaining cornmeal and chill, covered with plastic wrap, at least 1 hour or overnight. In a large heavy skillet heat the oil over medium-high heat until it is hot but not smoking and sauté the crab cakes in batches, turning them once, 3 to 4 minutes on each side, or until golden. As they are cooked, transfer them to paper towels to drain, then to baking sheets. Keep warm in a 200° oven. Serve warm with Tarragon Tartar Sauce and lemon wedges.

Makes 12 crab cakes.

Tarragon Tartar Sauce

1½ cups mayonnaise

3 shallots, minced

4 cornichons, minced

18 green olives, pitted and chopped

1½ tablespoons minced fresh tarragon leaves

1 tablespoon cider vinegar, or to taste

Tabasco to taste

Whisk all the ingredients together in a small bowl until combined well. Sauce can be made 1 day ahead and kept covered and chilled.

Makes about 2 cups.

Aunt Lena's Stuffed Sole
by Harry Stephens

Bella Luna, an Italian restaurant on Eastern Avenue, serves a special buffet on the Feast of the Seven Fishes, which takes place on Christmas Eve. Owner Harry Stephens says, "Stuffed sole was a treat for the holidays. My Aunt Lena made this dish and it was not something that was served during the course of the year."

1 bunch fresh spinach

½ cup ricotta

1 egg, beaten

2 tablespoons grated Parmesan

Pinch of nutmeg

Salt and pepper

4 fillets of sole

2 cups heavy cream

½ cup shredded mozzarella

Wash spinach. Without drying, put in a skillet with a lid and cook over medium heat until just cooked. Remove to a colander and squeeze out extra moisture. Chop. Mix ½ cup of the spinach with the ricotta, egg, Parmesan, nutmeg, salt and pepper. Spread this mixture on top of each fillet and roll it up like a cinnamon roll. Place them in a small baking pan where they fit snugly. Season the cream with a little salt and pepper; pour it over the fish. Top with the mozzarella and bake at 350° until the top is golden brown and the center of the rolled sole is hot.

Butter Cookies
by Shoshannah Hafner

Folks come from all over to experience the food prepared by Doug and Shoshannah Hafner at their Honey restaurant in Northside. Shoshannah has given us her favorite butter cookie recipe.

½ pound unsalted butter

1 cup superfine sugar

2 teaspoons vanilla, preferably Penzeys

1 large egg

1 large egg yolk

2½ cups flour

½ teaspoon French gray sea salt

1 tablespoon finely chopped candied ginger

1 teaspoon cinnamon, (Penzeys Vietnamese extra-fancy)

Fleur de sel

Raw sugar

Cream butter, sugar and vanilla. Add egg and egg yolk. Sift flour and sea salt together and add slowly, mixing just until combined. Stir in ginger and cinnamon. Roll dough into a log 1½ inches in diameter; wrap in parchment. Chill overnight, or 2 hours minimum. Slice cookies ¼ inch thick. Sprinkle with fleur de sel and raw sugar. Bake at 325° about 10 minutes.

Duck with Mushroom Polenta
by Jean-Robert de Cavel

The celebrated Cincinnati chef and restaurateur Jean-Robert de Cavel loves to cook the following dishes at Christmas because they are warm and inviting. Just reading the ingredients makes you want to get out the pots and pans. Bon appétit!

2 whole ducks

1 cup Woodford Reserve bourbon

1 medium onion, chopped

2 carrots, chopped

1 bouquet garni

4 sprigs fresh thyme

2 cups chicken stock

1 cup polenta cornmeal

Butter

½ cup heavy cream

8 ounces medley of shiitake, portobello and oyster mushrooms

2 shallots

1 bunch parsley

Olive oil

2 cups dark grapes

1½ tablespoons cracked black peppercorns

¼ cup honey

Red wine vinegar

½ cup grated Parmesan

Detach the legs and breasts from the ducks, reserving the legs and carcasses. Marinate the breasts in ½ cup of the bourbon for 2 hours in the refrigerator. Roast the carcasses at 400° for 40 minutes. Place the carcasses in a large saucepan or stockpot with the onion, carrots and bouquet garni. Deglaze roasting pan and add liquid to saucepan. Cover the carcasses with cold water, bring to a boil and reduce to a simmer. Simmer 1 hour. Skim stock. Strain stock; reduce to 3 cups.

Season the reserved duck legs with thyme, salt, pepper and a splash of the remaining bourbon. Roast them at 350° for 30 to 40 minutes, or until the meat falls off the bone. Shred the meat and cover with foil to keep warm.

Bring the 2 cups chicken stock to a boil. Add the cornmeal and cook 20 minutes. Add some butter and the cream. Salt and pepper to taste. Keep warm.

Cut all the mushrooms uniformly. Chop 1 shallot and the parsley. Sauté the mushrooms in olive oil; add the shallot and parsley. Salt and pepper to taste. Keep warm.

Cut each grape in half and sauté in butter until soft. Keep warm.

Chop the second shallot. Sauté it and 1 tablespoon of the cracked pepper in butter. Cook slowly. Add the honey. Cook until caramel consistency. Add a splash of the vinegar and the bourbon. Reduce by 75 percent. Add 2 cups of the duck stock, reducing if necessary. Add the grapes. Add some small pieces of butter to thicken. Salt to taste. Keep warm.

Heat oven to 375°. Season the duck breasts with salt and

pepper; sauté skin side down in an ovenproof pan over high heat on stovetop until golden, about 3 minutes. Turn breasts skin side up. Place pan in oven; roast 8 minutes for medium-rare. Remove from oven and cover with foil to keep warm.

Add mushroom mixture, the duck leg meat and the Parmesan to the polenta.

Place polenta on serving plate. Slice duck breasts and arrange on top. Ladle sauce over all. Serve warm.

Sea Bass with Mushroom Crust, Creamy Spinach, Roasted Pear and Pinot Noir Butter
by Jean-Robert de Cavel

3 bunches spinach

12 ounces white mushrooms

3 shallots

Olive oil

6 slices bacon

3 pears

2 sprigs parsley

10 ounces butter

1 bottle (750 milliliters) pinot noir

1 cup heavy cream

6 five-ounce sea bass

3 ounces shredded Parmesan

Mise en place: Clean the spinach and blanch in boiling water, then refresh in cold water; press dry. Chop the mushrooms and shallots; sauté in olive oil. Make duxelles by pureeing the mushroom–shallot mixture in a food processor; salt and pepper to taste. Dice, blanch and sauté the bacon. Cut 1 pear into 6 wedges; cut the other 2 pears into medium dice. In separate pans, toss the wedges and the dice with olive oil, salt and pepper to taste, and roast at 350° until cooked (dice will be done sooner). Chop the parsley. Dice the butter and return to refrigerator. Reduce the wine to ¼ cup. Reduce cream until thickened; keep warm.

Salt and pepper the fish and sauté in olive oil until halfway done, 2 to 4 minutes.

Add the parsley and Parmesan to the mushroom duxelles.

Add the spinach to the cream; add the diced pears and bacon. Salt and pepper to taste. Keep warm.

Place the mushroom duxelles on top of the fish and finish cooking in a 350° oven, 3 to 4 minutes.

Stir the butter into the wine. Salt and pepper to taste.

Place spinach mixture on serving plate. Arrange fish and pear wedges on top. Ladle with pinot noir butter.

Serves 6.

Photography Credits

Helen Adams, jacket photo of Jinny Berten

Jinny Berten, 59, 70, 72, 73, 86 left, 89 center, right, 97

Robert A Flischel, angels on back jacket, v, vii, ix, 34–36,
39–40, 53, 64–67, 87–89, 90–91, 106–107, 116

Phil Groshang, x

Peter Mueller, 80–81

Kelly Riccetti, 68–69, 71, 86 right

CK Wang of Wang News, 78–79

Tom Wolfe, 74–75

Sandy Underwood, 57, 84–85

Merry Christmas